REMEMBER YOU ARE DUST

Remember
You Are Dust

WALTER BRUEGGEMANN

edited by K. C. Hanson

CASCADE *Books* • Eugene, Oregon

REMEMBER YOU ARE DUST

Cascade Books
An Imprint of Wipf and Stock Publishers
199 W. 8th Ave., Suite 3
Eugene, OR 97401

www.wipfandstock.com

ISBN 13: 978-1-61097-535-3

Cataloging-in-Publication data:

Brueggemann, Walter.

    Remember you are dust / Walter Brueggemann ; edited by K. C.
Hanson.

    xii + 100 p.; 21.5 cm. Includes bibliographical references and indexes.

    ISBN 13: 978-1-61097-535-3

    1. Preaching. 2. Bible. O.T.—Homiletical use. I. Hanson, K. C. (Kenneth
C.). II. Title.

BS1191.5 B75 2012

Manufactured in the U.S.A.

Contents

Foreword

THIS IS THE SECOND volume of Walter Brueggemann's collected articles from *Journal of Preachers*, following on the heels of *Truth-telling as Subversive Obedience* (Cascade Books, 2011). I have prepared a unified bibliography and indexes to hopefully make the volume more accessible.

One finds in these essays many of the themes that Brueggemann has highlighted over the years in other writings, and readers who have read widely in his writings will recognize them: land (see *The Land: Place as Gift, Promise, and Challenge in Biblical Faith*, 2nd ed.), exile (see *Cadences of Home: Preaching among Exiles* and *Hopeful Imagination: Prophetic Voices in Exile*), and covenant (see *The Covenanted Self: Explorations in Law and Covenant*). But they offer fresh insights that develop out of these earlier works. I hope that you are as engaged by them as I have been.

K. C. Hanson

Preface

THE REPUBLICATION OF THESE articles in a collection makes clear to me two great debts that I have and am glad to acknowledge. On the one hand my blessed colleague, Erskine Clarke, as editor of the *Journal for Preachers*, invited me over time to submit these articles to the *Journal*. He had the intuitive sense of what it was possible and useful for me to do in the stream of my on-going thinking. On the other hand, K. C. Hanson has, in his tireless way, taken the initiative to gather these materials together in this collection. To both of these generous colleagues, I am abidingly grateful.

The collection, as it stands, is nicely framed by a prayer "against death" at the outset and a pondering of our humanity as "dust" in the concluding essay. The two together attend to the limited capacity of the human enterprise. The remarkable truth about gospel faith, however, is that such a recognition does not lead to immobilizing despair, nor does it lead to self-serving anxiety. Rather it leads, when faith is mature and critical, to glad submission of our life to the Easter God in obedience and in praise. The juxtaposition of obedience and praise (commented upon in these pages) stretches back to obedience in Psalm 1 and reaches forward to praise in Psalm 150; thus the Psalter, in its singing and praying, provides a taxonomy for a life of mature and critical faith. That juxtaposition keeps the church on the alert for two temptations. Praise keeps our life away for the reduction of mor-alistic obedience. Obedience keeps our lives anchored in Torah so that we do not float away in vacuous evangelical romanticism that smacks of New Age narcissism. Obedience and praise, taken together, turn our lives away from ourselves to the God who en-acts Easter impossibilities. And then they turn us back from that God to the fullness of our own lives in the presence of that God of impossibilities, that we may live in joy and confidence.

In these essays that reflect continuing preoccupation with the recurring themes of my thinking, I have written of exile, sub-version, and the seduction of modernity. I thought, as I wrote, that these were the right themes for careful attention. But now in retrospect, these summoning themes take on fresh urgency. Right before our very eyes, seemingly in a flash, we are watching the collapse of our long-held and long-trusted social infrastruc-ture. We are witnessing the deconstruction of faith claims and the dismantling of faith communities in the forms we have learned to assume and trust. Every preacher that I know comments on how abruptly and how deeply is the crisis of institutional faith. The reasons for that deconstruction and dismantling are many and complex, and no "blame game" will help us at all.

There are of course many possible outcomes of that disman-tling and deconstruction, and we can observe some of them. One of the obvious ones is that rising Christians in our society do not know and will not know of the disciplines that are required for the maintenance of a community of faith. No doubt many of the disciplines on which we have counted are passé; given that, it is nonetheless true that disciplines must be practiced so that the church is not just a community of convenience committed to private and passing religious impulses. The required disciplines, moreover, are rooted in theological acknowledgments that are presently out of vogue among us. The issue is not the survival of the institutional church. The issue, I suggest, is rather whether there will be sustained and sustainable communities of faith that can bear witness to the life of God in the world and to the life of the world lived in response to the God of the gospel. It is not very difficult to imagine the wholesale silencing of that witness.

Nor is it difficult to imagine the human costs of such a silencing. We can see signs and omens of a common life being resituated in the regime of money and power. In that world many, many will and are being "left behind," including some who mistakenly assumed they would benefit from such a silencing. We have now, in our society, become inured to the "propriety" of torture. As I write this, moreover, we are presently being assured by our government that "drone attacks" on targeted persons are "legal." We are, at the same time that we prattle about "security" watching the programmatic dismantling of any sustainable "safety net" in the interest of greater concentrations of money and power in the hands of the few. Such manipulation of the common good always evokes the sounds of the displaced (exiles), always invites subversion, and always ponders how to survive, always ask yet again to whom the land belongs.

Clearly faithful gospel witness in such a lethal social system requires deep prayer and candor about the limit of credible hubris, but also critical thinking that has a significant bite beyond familiar sound bytes. It is my modest hope that these reprinted pieces may make a contribution to that task of faith and ministry that becomes increasingly urgent among us.

Walter Brueggemann

1

The Last Enemy Is Death

BIBLICAL FAITH IS, OF course, resolutely covenantal, with both parties—God and God's people—deeply engaged in interactive communication with each other. That covenantal dialogue of engagement, moreover, is conducted in the conviction that utterance to the partner does impact the partner in important ways. That is, such communication is, according to biblical faith, genuine engagement. Harold Fisch, in resisting the temptation that such faithful utterance is mere subjectivity, judges:

> This becomes an article of faith for D. Robertson, who declares that "the Israelite community knows what Shelley knows, that no petition from them is going to lead God to make human life basically different." This is *not* what the Israelite community knows: it knows that, mysterious though the ways of God are, there is still a potency in prayer, a power not to be rigidly separated from outer events in the "world"—"this poor man cried and the Lord heard, and saved him out of all his troubles" (34:6) . . . Against the purity of the inner dialogue, or rather in addition to it, we have the emphasis repeated here, as in many other psalms, on the comforts of the Temple worship, where the well-tried and well-established forms

1

of ritual observance bring to the dialogue with God an
institutional basis and framework.[1]

The meeting between God and God's people is precisely for such
interaction.

Given such a dialogic assumption, it is conventional that
God's word to God's people is in the sermon (the burden of the
preacher) *and the word of God's people to God* is in prayer. For
the most part, that seems a responsible and adequate way to understand the dialogue. It is clear, however, that the *word of the
sermon* tends to be proclaimed with much more authority and
clarity than the word of God's people to God in prayer, so that the
communication tends to be quite one-sided; in such a practice the
word of God's people in prayer may become so deferential and
mute that it does not hold up its end of the transaction.

For that reason, I have suggested that on occasion it is appropriate in preaching that the preacher should not address the
church with God's word, but the sermon might well be "our turn"
to speak the word of the church that might be addressed even
to God. Such an articulation might be especially appropriate in
times of bewilderment and deep anxiety when a clear word from
God is not readily available. Such communal utterance via the
pastor might be an occasion for candor that in turn creates an
environment of receptivity for what might then be uttered of the
gospel.

I suspect that in the cluster of circumstances stretching from
9/11 to the self-indulgent U.S. invasion of Iraq, there might be
a circumstance for such a slot on preaching. On such an occasion, the preacher might well voice the bewilderment and anxiety,
the anger and confusion, as well as the faith of the church. In the
sermon that follows, Ralph Hawkins has done just such a daring
act to bring to speech the mix of faith and fear that character-
izes the people of God. Every preacher knows that our present

---

1. Fisch, *Poetry with a Purpose*, 110–11.

circumstance is a strenuous venue for preaching. The purpose of such a sermon, I take it, is not to duck the risky work of proclamation, but to recognize that the church meets in a deep season of unresolved. Such candor is an important component of faith, a public acknowledgment of the crisis of faith, precisely the arena in which God's spirit may make things new.

∼

In the tradition of the psalmists, in such prayers as Psalm 102, and in the spirit of their vocation as language-crafters and prayer-makers for the priestly people of God, I humbly offer the following psalm[2] as an interpretation of the Word and as our speech to God in these troubled days:

> To you, O Father of Grace, we lift our voices;
> to you, Creator of Life, we speak our supplications.
>> Do not hide your face from us
>> in this day of our distress.
>> Turn your ear our way;
>> answer us with haste as we cry out.
>> Ours is a life filled with anxiety;
>> we are a people full of dread.

> Into a sanctuary of gospel grace we have gathered; from a world of relentless violence we have come. All around us are deeds of arrogance and anger; revenge and more revenge are our neighbors:

---

2. Much of the language and style for this psalm comes from the following sources: Psalm 102; 1 Corinthians 15; Matt 5:9, and the Presbyterian *Brief Statement of Faith* (1984).

old wounds opened
cultures clashed
planes hijacked
towers felled
anthrax found
troops sent out
hills/caves hunted
plastic/tape procured
threat colors adopted
war now engineered.

We are this day like a people torn in two: Our hearts are here with you in praise; our minds are all over the world in fear.

As tanks line up and missiles depart,
as canisters turn up and plots are revealed,
it is now clear again:
Our days are like the evening shadow;
we wither away so easily, like dry grass.

But you, O Lord, are enthroned forever; your good name endures despite such threats.

You and you alone have made us image-bearers.
You have made us female and male,
neighbors in our imaged humanity;
even us, made covenant people by your grace.

You spoke and the world gladly came to be . . .
You brought the creation safely across the waters . . .
You called old men and old women to make new life . . .
You made in them a contract to bless the world . . .
You brought your children out of pyramid-bondage.

We were often confused to see you make wars of old,
for we thought you were the God of life.

But then, in the fullness of your time,
you confirmed our glad suspicions:
You and you alone sent your Peacemaker;
you delivered unto us the fullness of who you are.
Now we guess and conjecture no longer;
now your will is as clear as his good face.

You have been the kind maker of the world,
Father to an eternal nation of your graced people.
Come to our aid again;
create new life among us once more.
Rise up and have compassion on our world,
now so torn asunder with
our deathly machines
our deathly wills
our deathly times

You do not desire more war;
more calculated death is not your aim.
Soften hearts and minds with your peace;
obstruct war games with your destiny.
Come and destroy your last grand enemy:
make death itself your final spoil.

To you, O Christ now risen, we lift our voices;
to you, O Savior of life, we speak our supplications.
Yours is now a resurrected life
and you have put us on that path.
You live with the Father in everlasting life;
we live with each other in mounting threat.
Your wounds are rich, yet now not deathly;
our wounds abound, now threatening war.

In your resurrection state,
    come and enact your ministry among us again:
    preach again good news to the poor
    release again the captives of this world
    teach us again God-ways by word and deed
    bless the children and even your enemies
    heal the sick and bind up the brokenhearted
    eat with outcasts and forgive stubborn sinners.

    Are we to do these things for you?
    Surely your kingdom then will fall! What is the middle
way, O Christ? What is the faithful action in this hour?
    Outright war runs counter to your peace;
benign inaction seems foolish and naive. What is the kingdom
way, O Christ? What is the calling of your graced people?

But this we know well:
    God raised you, O Christ, from the dead,
    vindicating your sinless life,
    breaking the power of our evil,
    delivering us across the water,
    from death to life anew.

    Now, in your foolish ways,
you have made us your covenant people:
    church
    holy nation
    called-out ones
    order of priests.

So priests we will be,
with our halting prayers.

We love this nation, this America of liberty,
but still we know that we are citizens of your heaven.
We are baptized *into your* eternal nation,
and so we pray to you in our in-between state:
one foot on the ground of a united states,
another foot on the soil of your resurrection home.

In your kingdom-teaching your instructions came down;
your edict for life with you in heaven is hauntingly clear:
"pray for your enemies,"
lift up to God their lives and yours.
So let this be recorded for a generation to come,
so that a people yet unborn may praise you O Christ,
that you looked down from your holy height,
from resurrection life you looked to earth
to stifle the terror that so fills the people,
to cut off the need for war-making plans.
Resurrection life is your agenda;
death and its agents are your last enemy.

O Christ of the kingdom way, redeem our enemies:
Osama
Saddam
Al-Qaeda
and their many friends of destruction.

Invade their deathly kingdoms
with your kingdom of life.
You are the prince of peace;
you are the Lord of all new things.
As it was said of old:
"you must reign until you have put all his enemies under your
feet. The last enemy to be destroyed is death."

O Resurrected One,
    destroy it now.

To you, O Spirit Holy, we lift our voices,
to you, Sustainer of Life, we speak our supplications.

You call us *church*;
    you make us a people in Christ.
    But we are timid and lame:
    we trust our defenses
    we worship our securities
    we shore up our safety.

We need your power to sustain our kingdom calling; we require
your presence to live like God's people,
    for we dwell in a land betwixt and between:
    full of freedom, full of sin.

This land sets us free for your purposes,
and we are grateful.
This land offers its children to protect such a liberty,
and we are honored.
This land offers protections from threats all around,
and we are secured.
This land defends our peculiar call to live as New Covenant
people, and so we hope to live well, as the baptized ones.
    Hear these, our words of gratitude.

But certainly you must also know
    that this land affords its own evil,
    this nation harbors its own sins.
    And so we need your quickening power.

We are often too strong for faith
    often too cynical for hope
    often too preoccupied for love.
    We are too wealthy for sacrificing crosses;
    we are too enlightened for resurrection hope.

But you, Sprit of God, Holy Presence of Christ,
you are everywhere the giver and renewer of life:
    you grace us through faith
    you give us liberty in God
    you sustain a land with law
    you bind us together as a churchly people.

Certainly you can then again blow your winds;
    certainly you can renew the mess of our world.

Hover over the lands of our enemies
and birth in them today
    new life
    new peace
    new hope
    new rule
    new trust
    in the one true God of life.

Brood over the lands we call our temporary home,
and birth in this nation
    new faith
    new restraint
    new kindness
    new humility
    new trust
    in the only Lord of life.
In a broken and fearful world,
you give us the courage

to pray without ceasing . . .
to witness among all neighbors near and far. . .
to unmask idolatries in church and state . . .
to hear the voices of peoples long silenced . . .
to work with others for justice, freedom, and peace.

Send down your Courage this day.
Blow among us with Pentecost power.
Death shall not abide.
Spirit winds will surely blow.

Oh, how we long for resurrection life!
Oh, how we can see it now in our hearts!

Oh, how we pray that what has begun in First Fruits
will be brought to completion here and now, among us!
O God of such new-life-power,
We long to worship and serve again
with those brothers and sisters we have lost.
We long for a time when guns
will be traded for bread.
We long for a time when our ships of battle
will be scrapped for arks of grace.
We long for a season when war
will give way to friendship.
Then we will worship with you, and you will be all in all!

We hear the scoffers all around and in us:
Unrealistic! Pie-in-the-sky! Impossible!
But so is Easter morning.
Yet you raised him again to new life.
Wonderfully impossible!
Amaze us again.

Father, Son, Holy Spirit:

"You must reign until you have put all his enemies under your feet. The last enemy to

be destroyed is death."

Destroy it now.

Amen.

2

Praise to God Is the End of Wisdom— What Is the Beginning?

WISDOM CULMINATES IN PRAISE! Wisdom of course is not the acquiring of knowledge nor the accumulation of data. It is long-term, patient, discerning attentiveness to the character and quality of life, to the sustaining inter-relations that appear, to the peculiar ways in which life comes to fruition, in which promises are kept, in which pathologies cost, in which healings happen.[1] Such attentiveness may be discerned in the largeness of creation, in the delicacy of a birth, in the mystery of self. Such attentiveness is not blind to evil, brutality, and death; in the midst of such powerful realities, nonetheless, wise attentiveness is pressed beyond life observed, finally to say, "Thou."[2] Regard for creation urges us to the creator whom we address in wonder, awe, amazement,

---

1. The basic and most helpful book on wisdom is von Rad, *Wisdom in Israel*. The most helpful introduction is Crenshaw, *Old Testament Wisdom: An Introduction*. See also Crenshaw, ed., *Studies in Ancient Israelite Wisdom*.

2. This culmination is evident in Psalm 150, which simply "enjoys" God, and in Job 42:1–6 in which Job finally yields to the overwhelming reality of God with whom he now communes.

and gratitude.[3] The ultimate expression of our attentiveness, the conclusion drawn, does not lead to a scientific formulation, to an intellectual conclusion, or to technical certainty, but to lyrical self-abandonment. Such attentiveness leads finally to doxology, to the ceding of life in its wonder and gratitude over to the one who is its progenitor, sponsor, and sovereign.

Wisdom Begins in Obedience

Praise is where wisdom ends.[4] Wisdom, however, does not automatically and in every case end there. Wisdom ends in doxology, only if long-term, patient, discerning attentiveness begins in the right way at the right place. In order to end in praise, wisdom must begin in obedience. A biblical way of speaking of this point of embarkation is this: "Fear of Yahweh is the beginning of wisdom" (Prov 9:10; cf. 1:7; Ps 111:10).[5] The purpose of this paper is to explore the intention of that biblical formula, and to consider its importance for our situation of life and ministry.

The testimony of the Bible is unambiguous. Believing persons are to learn to "fear God."[6] The phrase "fear God" is elusive, and for that reason misleading. It seems to include the notion of dread and terror before God. Because dread and terror are too heavy, however, our propensity is to speak instead of awe, wonder, and reverence. I suspect that the phrase intends to include in its scope a great range of nuances that run from terror to wonder. If we try to articulate all of these nuances in a single affirmation, we may suggest that "fear of God" means to take God *with utmost seriousness* as the premise and perspective from which life is to be

3. See especially Zimmerli, "The Place and Limit of Wisdom."

4. Miller writes: "The praise of God is the last word of faith. It is our 'end' in life, the end or goal toward which all our life is set. All the songs and prayers of Israel contained in the Psalter reach their final climax in praise. In praise, therefore, God gives *us* the last word" ("In Praise and Thanksgiving," 188).

5. On this theme, see von Rad, *Wisdom in Israel*, 53–73.

6. Von Rad comments: "The statement that the fear of the Lord was the beginning of wisdom was Israel's most special possession" (ibid., 68).

discerned and lived. That "utmost seriousness" requires attentiveness to some things rather than others, to spend one's energies in response to this God who has initiated our life. While a variety of texts might be cited that illuminate this phrase, I will mention four texts that give some flavor to the phrase.

> 1. Do not fear, for God has come to prove you, and that the fear of him may be before your eyes, that you may not sin. (Exod 20:20)

This text is placed immediately after the Ten Commandments at Mt. Sinai. Thus the sentence surely is a summons to obedience, that is, obedience to the commandments just given. It is through obedience to the commandments that Israel fears God and does not sin. Notice though that the summons to fear in the mouth of Moses begins with the invitation, "Do not fear."[7] The fear as obedience to which Israel is summoned is not terror and dread, but responsiveness to God's will. Israel's life is to be lived in responsiveness to God's will, and that will is given in the commandments.

> 2. For Yahweh your God is testing you to know whether you love Yahweh your God with all your heart and with all your soul. You shall walk after Yahweh your God and fear him, and keep his commandments and obey his voice, and you shall serve him and cleave to him. (Deut 13:3–4)

The teaching of Deuteronomy is an exposition of the Sinai text. Deuteronomy loves to pile up words so that "fear" is treated as a parallel to "love, walk after, keep, listen (obey), serve, and cleave." Clearly the emphasis is upon attending to God's will and not upon dread and terror.

Deuteronomy, moreover, knows in remarkable detail about the will of Yahweh and what constitutes fear and obedience. Deuteronomy is the great biblical statement on *covenanting* as a way of ordering all social relations. In the vision of society offered

---

7. On the phrase "fear not," see Conrad, *Fear Not Warrior*.

in this text, in every aspect of life—political, economic, military, judicial, and familial—members of the community are bound in care to each other. They are bound not only to God but to the neighbor, the strong to the weak, the powerful to the vulnerable and needy. "Fear of God" then is not a cognitive operation but it is a premise from which to shape social relations in a certain way. This way of social relations is diametrically opposed to Canaanite ways that this tradition views as idolatrous, destructive, and deathly. "Fear of God" is a summons to disengage from modes of social relationships that not only alienate from Yahweh, but also from neighbor.

> 3. The fear of Yahweh is the beginning of wisdom,
> and the knowledge of the Holy One is insight. (Prov 9:10)

At first glance, the instruction in Proverbs is very different from the imperative of Deuteronomy. If, however, one reads more closely, it becomes apparent that Proverbs, like Deuteronomy, is interested in the resilient way in which the several parts of society are related to each other, indeed, the way in which parts of creation are related to each other. The wisdom teacher has observed that certain deeds yield certain consequences.[8] Certain choices inevitably produce certain results. The rule of Yahweh has ordered creation so that those connections persist and cannot be circumvented.[9] There are reliable patterns of relationship that cannot be mocked or voided. Attention to those reliable patterns finally leads one to marvel at the God who has so ordered life. Wisdom is the habit of observing these interrelations, honoring them, and accepting them as the terms of one's life. Wisdom thus is the awareness that the world is not endlessly pliable, but that God has ordered in the very fabric of creation a system of gifts and costs that must be treated seriously. In sum, wisdom is the acknowledgment that God's terms for living will prevail, and that

8. Koch, "Is There a Doctrine of Retribution in the Old Testament?"

9. See especially Zimmerli, "The Place and Limit of Wisdom"; and Zimmerli, "Concerning the Structure of Old Testament Wisdom."

when honored, they yield well-being, and when mocked, they bring trouble.[10]

> 4. Blessed is the man who fears Yahweh,
> who greatly delights in his commandments (Ps 112:1)

Notice that Ps 112:1 places in parallel "fear of God" and "commandments," respectively the categories of Proverbs (fear) and Deuteronomy (commandments). The two modes of articulation (wisdom and covenant) are brought together.[11] The remainder of this psalm explicates the conduct of the God-fearer as one who practices righteousness and justice, who is generous, stable, liberal, and caring. His life is attuned to the generous, caring righteousness of God's own practice, which is explicated in Psalm 111.

From these several texts there emerges a model of human life that lives out in daily practice the caring for all parts of creation that belong to God's will for the world. The seriousness of the mandate embraced by this human agent has not eliminated the terror and dread of the requirement, but has transposed terror and dread into positive acts of life-enhancement. Wisdom is the lived conviction that life lived in certain terms and ways (terms and ways I would term "covenantal") leads to well-being. Wisdom is the awareness that these ways are nonnegotiable, and that the embrace of these ways is right, proper, good, appropriate, and joyous. A life that begins in such awareness and embrace surely will end in doxology. Conversely, a life that rejects this awareness and refuses this embrace will end without praise. There will be no one to praise and no will to sing.

---

10. This moral "settlement" of reality, so well articulated in Psalm 37, of course will not hold in the face of recalcitrant data. It is for that reason that the poetry of Job challenges the moral "settlement" on which conventional wisdom rests.

11. The linkage between commandment and wisdom has been shrewdly explored by Gerstenberger in *Wesen and Herkunft des apodiktischer Rechts*; he proposes that the commandments at the center of the torah are derivative in form from the admonitions and prohibitions of wisdom instruction.

Four Affirmations

From this brief sketch we may articulate four affirmations that belong to a practice of the fear of God:

1. "Fear of God" is not cowering, frightened intimidation. Those who fear God are not wimps and are not preoccupied with excessive need to please God. They are rather those who have arrived at *a fundamental vision of reality about life with God*, who have enormous power, freedom, and energy to live out that vision. "Fear of God" is liberating and not restrictive, because it gives confidence about the true shape of the world.

2. "Fear of God" *concerns ethical praxis*, the actual doing of a certain kind of life. The obedience that the phrase enjoins, however, is not the endless pursuit of rules, so that obedience is reduced to excessive scrupulosity. Rather this obedience is the embrace and enactment of a vision of reality, a vision that shapes every social relationship and transaction. Wisdom is the capacity to see how this vision of reality is present in and operative through every moment of *praxis*.

3. "Fear of God" is not a collection of little commandments and of detailed insights about this and that. Rather, it is the courageous capacity to insist that all of *life has a moral coherence* and a unity of purpose and meaning. Wisdom is the daring affirmation that all of life is better understood and more truly discerned in relation to God's governance and sovereignty. That governance maintains expectation for every social relation, and no part of life is remote from that large sovereignty. Wisdom then is the readiness to see and enter into all of life as an area where God's will is decisive.

4. The accent on *praxis*, on doing God's will, should not weaken our recognition that wisdom is *an intellectual, epistemological enterprise*. Wisdom concerns not only doing, but also

knowing. Wisdom is an intellectual premise for living life, an elemental acknowledgment that life derives from and is accountable to God. Wisdom then is not a frantic effort to arrive at a proper theological conclusion, but it is the confident embrace of a theological premise and assumption. Life does not finally add up to wisdom, but wisdom is the assumption from which life is adequately and faithfully lived. Thus "fear of Yahweh is the beginning of wisdom" is a decision that *faith seeks understanding.*[12] This initial discernment of God's sovereign intentionality illuminates every aspect of our living. We come at life already knowing.

Clearly it is this perception of life that we crave for our children. There is no doubt that "fear of Yahweh" has been variously used to intimidate, as a form of social control, and as a defense for certain preferred customs and practices. We have all too easily equated our particular way with "fear of God." Underneath all such distorted uses, however, it is clear that this pervasive premise from the Bible insists on a coherent, unified, liberating, theocentric vision of human life and of all creation. For all its problematic character, this affirmation makes a qualitative and decisive difference in our living.

Modernity's Challenge

Without knowing exactly why, we sense in our bones that this presentation of reality holds thin authority among us. This biblical vision of human faith and conduct is now scarcely credible, and when we speak it, we tone it down in order not to be ludicrous. The reasons for this lack of credibility are complicated and

12. On the programmatic significance of the practice of faith seeking understanding, see Barth, *Fides Quaerens Intellectum*; and Cushman, *Faith Seeking Understanding*. It is impossible to overstate the significance of this posture for a right understanding of theology. In contemporary theology, this conviction is reflected in the work of Hans Frei and George Lindbeck.

far from clear. They have to do, in any case, not with some recent emergence of "permissiveness," or the "breakdown of the family," or any of the easy targets of blame. Rather we are heirs of a long intellectual process that is in deep conflict with the biblical vision, and that continues to offer a powerful and attractive alternative vision of reality. It will be valuable for our teaching and preaching to recognize that we articulate a vision of reality that is at deep odds with the dominant intellectual assumptions of our culture.

The dominant alternative to a biblical vision (which we may term "modernity") has roots that go back to the Renaissance and Reformation, which came along with the rise of science and became dominant with the positivism of the Enlightenment. This entire intellectual development, of which we are the inescapable heirs, has championed unfettered autonomy and has regarded any authoritative tradition as its enemy and as the enemy of autonomous freedom. If we are to locate the intellectual underpinnings of that modernist perspective, we may attend especially to the work of Descartes and Locke, though the development of modernity is more complex than the identification of any particular names. Descartes has introduced us to the principle of doubt as the most honest intellectual activity we can undertake. Locke has shaped us to believe that the unit of social meaning and agency is the individual person, without reference to community or tradition. It is clear that doubt and autonomy do not cohere in any way with the vision of reality encoded as "fear of Yahweh." Indeed the faith of Israel intended to counter doubt with its appeal to authoritative torah. Its response to any notion of individual autonomy was the prior claim of the community. *Authoritative teaching* and *priority of community* are central aspects of biblical faith that are resisted and countered by the modernity of Descartes and Locke.

In my reading I have found the following four statements helpful in understanding the alien intellectual climate in which evangelical faith must now be practiced:

1. Crawford McPherson, *The Political Theory of Possessive Individualism*[13] has shown how Lockean individualism has reshaped and redefined our sense of self, so that our personhood is not embedded in an affirmative tradition, but depends upon aggressive, individual self-securing through getting and consuming. This discernment of human reality has made getting and having the goal of human existence. It takes no great imagination to see that such possessive individualism evokes values of satiation and self-assertiveness that show up in every area of life, including economics and sexuality.

2. Karl Polyani, *The Great Transformation*,[14] has traced the way in which the power of the "market" has been slowly and decisively detached from the fabric of social relations. "The economy" became an autonomous force in the modern world, without attachment to or responsibility for social relations. While Polyani's historical analysis does not score the point, the connection between autonomous economy and unbridled consumerism is not difficult to imagine. The "pay-out" of such an autonomous practice of economy is that one can hear Margaret Thatcher speaking of the market as though it were a personal agent, as in "the market knows best."

3. Alasdair MacIntyre, *Whose Justice? Which Rationality?*[15] has provided a shrewd critique of the theory of justice contained in "liberalism," by which he means the justice of the free market system of individual autonomy. Though it lies beyond MacIntyre's analysis, it is easy to notice that the unbridled character of the nation-state in the modern world easily coheres with such a diminishment of any sense

13. MacPherson, *The Political Theory of Possessive Individualism*.
14. Polanyi, *The Great Transformation*.
15. MacIntyre, *Whose Justice? Which Rationality?*

of comprehensive relatedness of social relations. MacIntyre makes the point that every view of justice is embedded in historical experience, and that even "liberalism" that understands itself positivistically is also the product of a history and needs to be critiqued on that basis.[16]

4. Lesslie Newbigin, *Foolishness to the Greeks*,[17] has more popularly considered the disappearance of teleological purpose from social transactions in the face of technological positivism. When such purpose has been completely denied, then all relations are reduced to technical operations in which human worth and dignity are compromised, disregarded, and often destroyed. Modernity is committed to the denial of any purpose beyond the chosen, expressed purpose of those involved in the transaction.

These brief comments about the character of modernity are of course much too thin, for I have reported on areas of study beyond my expertise. It may be sufficient, however, to suggest: a) this is an important literature to which ministers must attend; b) the disappearance of "fear of God" from our lips and our lives is not accidental or incidental, but it is massive and programmatic; c) there is no ground of accommodation between a biblical vision of reality and that of modernity; d) the causes of this profound tension and enormous loss are not to be located in any of the easy "whipping boys" of religious rhetoric; and, therefore, e) recovery and fresh affirmation of a biblical vision of reality will not be arrived at easily or simply. My comments intend only to make the point that we are participants in an enormous cultural shift that has powerful intellectual underpinnings. It is, in my judgment, worth a great deal to understand what lies behind the behaviors and responses that on the surface seem simply indifferent and irresponsible.

16. Ibid., 326–69.
17. Newbigin, *Foolishness to the Greeks*.

Thus my thesis is in two parts:

1. While always living at the edge of authoritarianism, the theme of "fear of God" articulated a unified, coherent ordering of life and urged attentiveness to and responsibility for the quality of social transactions.

2. The dominant values of modernity (which are marked by autonomy, secularization, and individualism) aim at social relations that are reduced to technique, at a quality of life that is finally profane, and at a character of personhood that is reduced to commodity.

The life sponsored and endorsed by modernity clearly succeeds as obedience is banished from life's beginning, and praise is precluded at its end. Without a beginning in obedience or an end in praise, human life becomes only a mid-term holding action marked by despair and anxiety, generating fear, and frequently slipping into brutality.

An Anguished Pathos

I have stated these matters as clearly as I know how. Indeed, the reader may think, this is a caricature, and may conclude that there is middle ground between the two views, middle ground that I do not recognize. Obviously the trajectory of modernity seldom is acted out in such extreme form. It is more visible in mindless consumerism, in an endless pursuit of a "higher standard of living," in a blind passion for capital punishment, in gang rapes and their various social justifications, in a military budget that lacks rationality in the name of "deterrence," in political discourse that avoids the human issues of hurt and hope, in a redefinition of human personhood as consumer and commodity, in a yearning for religious voices that will conform the gospel to these several pathologies. For many people, the deep threat and pain of this crisis is the awareness that their children can no longer relate to the great claims of the faith, not because they are rebellious, but because they do not care, or caring, cannot understand or see the point. They no longer know where responsible social passion comes from, why caring is important, or how the disciplines of faith matter, or why. There is, between parents and children, a common yearning marked partly by a helpless apathy and partly by an anguished pathos. The yearning arises not because anyone is "bad," but because an alien perception of reality makes engagement with the tradition of "fear of Yahweh" unconvincing and without credibility.

Pastoral Responsibility

Thus far I have tried to characterize the deep claims of the old tradition of "fear of God" and to state why "God" has disappeared and "fear" has become so odd and so scarce among us. I wish now to comment on our pastoral responsibility in that context.

There are several things we are tempted to do that we must not do:

1. We must not engage in too much nostalgia for how it used to be, for it used to be authoritarian. In any case, moreover, modernity has given us great gifts that should not be discounted.

2. We must not engage in too much browbeating about the losses, as in "Where did we go wrong?" Such a worry is a little like asking, "Who lost China?" when in fact China has never been lost. Perhaps Constantinian Christendom needed to be "lost."

3. We must not try quick fixes, to give a veneer or fraudulent replication of the good old days. This is the temptation of right-wing religion with its shrill insistence on doctrinal accuracy or moral correctness. The issues are much more dense and deep, and such efforts only commit us to a cover-

up of the real problems. The issues in the crisis of modernity do not concern simply morality or orthodoxy, but a promise of faith that dares to see reality as a moral unity.

4. We must not try excessive accommodation to tailor our Christianity to modernity. This is the temptation of the left under the guise of "pluralism," which most often turns out to mean simply "to each her own."

When we are not staggered by our situation or excessively compromised, we may find energy to celebrate the urgency of the pastoral, teaching, interpreting task of the church. We have entrusted to us a vision of reality that is a formidable and healthy response to the pathology of modernity, if we can keep our faith, our sense, and our cool. The articulation and offer of this evangelical alternative will require hard intellectual work to give voice to a vision that lies outside the conventions and categories of our culture.

It is, I submit, important to recognize our true cultural situation (which pertains even if we are in the "Bible belt" and blessed with a kind of Presbyterian buoyancy). The truth is that we are committed to a vision of reality that is deeply at odds with the modernity, autonomy, individualism that is embraced by most conservatives, by most liberals, and mostly by us. This means, I suggest, that our task is subversive, sectarian, and counterculture, and that task requires different awarenesses and different expectations, both of ourselves and of others.

1. The pastoral task of the church is *subversive*. This subversive does not have to do in any first sense with social action. It has to do with the subversion of the imagination of modernity. Children of modernity do not imagine that they imagine. And when we imagine, we imagine that we are simply objective in our discernment. Even when we do not imagine that we imagine, we do nonetheless. We imagine we are free, unfettered agents. Our subversion of such a sense of autonomy

is to notice that we are embedded in a *remembered tradition*, and that we are embedded in a *structured creation* that has its own say.[18] Both remembered tradition and structured creation give us gifts and both hold us deeply accountable. The work of subversion is to summon people to be ill-fitted and ill-suited for the modernity around us, so that we have the freedom and grace to construe ourselves as children who receive, and not as technicians who devise or as automatons who process.

2. The pastoral task of the church is *sectarian*.[19] Since Troeltsch stacked the cards, the term "sect" has been a negative word, referring to religious kooks. Rightly understood and free of the sociology of European Christianity, the term refers to an intentional religious community that proposes and practices a vision of reality not respected or embraced by the dominant culture. The "sect-work" of the American church is not primarily issue-oriented (e.g., war, sexuality, economics), nor is it ideologically of the right or of the left. Rather that work has to do with the main claim of the faith that "fear of God" begins wisdom, that obedience begets a true discernment of reality. The sect offers an alternative and expects that this alternative may win adherents and gain credibility for a redefinition of public life. "Sectarian" does not mean withdrawal, but the voicing of an alternative that calls to radical repentance concerning public reality.

---

18. MacIntyre has shown how even the imagined situation of being unfettered and autonomous is in fact a situation of being embedded in a tradition. The imagined situation is an illusion. The juxtaposition of *remembered tradition* and *structured creation* is intended to refer in the Old Testament to, respectively, the creedal recital and to the teaching of wisdom. In both modes, torah and wisdom, the notion of autonomy is of course denied.

19. On a positive reading of "sectarian," see Hauerwas, "Will the Real Sectarian Stand Up?"; and Brueggemann, "II Kings 18–19: The Legitimacy of a Sectarian Hermeneutic."

3. The pastoral task of the church is *counter-cultural.* This term of course does not mean beads, long hair, and dropouts. It means that we affirm and enact a counter-vision of social relations, counter to the greedy brutality now so much in vogue. The memory of the church in Scripture provides a language that means to counter the dominant language. As we seriously and imaginatively engage that "second" language, that language will begin to spill into the central human issues.

The preacher (and the church) are entrusted with a vision of reality rooted in sovereignty, enacted in concrete social transactions, sustained by old memories, and powered by long hopes. That vision of reality must be sounded in its grand scope, but mostly it is mediated in lesser ways, a day at a time, a text at a time, a sacrament at a time. In our context, I submit that this subversive, sectarian, countercultural enterprise has to do with practice of public language around the reality of *human hurt and human hope.* These are realities that are mostly lost in the shuffle with our talk of security, affluence, freedom, and power.

The biblical tradition, however, found *hurt and hope* the irreducible human factors. Moreover, it found the drama of *human hurt* enacted in the crucifixion of Jesus, and the drama of *human hope* realized in the resurrection of Jesus. When the church fixes its language on hurt and hope, the great issues of public life and of personal identity get redefined. We begin to notice that hurt and hope reshape our unbridled freedom to "do my own thing." We sense that our passion for private property is not so innocent. It occurs to us that our indulgence and satiation in consumer goods and sexuality are not as central as we imagined. We think again about the failure of financial and military power to make secure, the inability of might to make right, and the incapacity of greed to bring joy.

What is needed among us, I sense, is the slow, steady, sustained, conviction that this evangelical vision of reality about "the fear of God" matters and will prevail. We are indeed embedded people, and all the modernity in the world cannot undo that reality. Our worship is an affirmation of our particular embeddedness. Our ethic is the enactment of that embeddedness. Our faith is the naming of the One who gives us our long-term habitat, identity, and vocation.

A Summit Meeting

As I thought about writing this piece and pastors reading it, I imagined we could all be silent observers at a summit meeting between the biblical vision and that of modernity. The summit meeting is hosted by Moses (who else?) and is attended by the doubting of Descartes and the possessing of Locke. René and John find the meeting odd. They do not understand the conversation and they do not want to be there. Moses, however, is a wonderful host who will not permit them to leave; Moses has too many stories to tell. He regales them with Pharaohs confronted, with double bread given for sabbath, with tablets received, and calves crushed. Then Moses takes his resistant friends to the brink of Pisgah and shows them the land where they have never been, milk and honey—all in promise. The conversation is difficult, because Descartes has no memory and Locke has no hope. Moses nonetheless insists on his version of reality, meal after meal, tale after tale, wonder after wonder.

Moses is such a free person in his present moment and one wonders why. It is because Moses knows so much. He remembers so much. He remembers that his life is rooted in obedience. That is where it all began:

> His delight is in the torah of Yahweh,
> > on his torah he meditates day and night.
> He is like a tree
> > planted by streams of water. (Ps 1:2–3)

Moses also recalls that he is headed to the land of praise, where he
will stand unencumbered with timbrel and pipe. He will sing with
Israel and with angels:

> Praise Yahweh!
> Praise God in God's sanctuary;
>> praise him in his mighty firmament!
> Praise him for God's mighty deeds
>> praise him according to his surpassing greatness. (Ps 150:1)

Moses is so very sure about the beginnings in *obedience* and the
ending in *praise*. He is therefore not tense about the present,
not worried about its outcome. He is utterly free and, therefore,
threatening to us and winsome. Moses' exchange with Descartes
and Locke is tough; we do not know if Moses will prevail because
the meeting is not yet completed.

We do know this much. As the conversation goes on with
the devisors of modernity, notice that "the fear of Yahweh" is not
a careless slogan or a dumb moralism. It is an allusion to another
whole way of life, rooted in the reality of God's purpose. René and
John may still go their way in doubt and acquisitiveness. Moses,
however, yields nothing and concedes nothing, for he believes his
vision of reality is rooted in the character of God, who will not
be banished. That God has a holy and terrible name (Ps 111:9),
a name issuing commands, authorizing songs, giving life, never
conceding, or yielding, or failing.[20] We observe the meeting, un-
observed. Then it dawns on us that this is our meeting too, along
with the holy terrible name, and Moses and all the saints. This
company always starts again at the beginning, in obedience.

20. On the God who saves and commands, see Fackenheim, *God's
Presence in History: Jewish Affirmations and Philosophical Reflections*, 14–19
and passim.

3

The "Turn" from Self to God

PSALM 77 OFFERS A stunning embodiment of the reorientation of life most hoped for by evangelical faith. In the exposition that follows, I take the psalm not simply as a devotional or liturgical residue of faith, but as an actual "speech pilgrimage" of one whose self spoke through to new faith. Specifically, the psalm shows the route by which this life was moved from a *preoccupation with self* to a *submission to and reliance upon God.*

Self-concern

The first part of the psalm is a fairly standard complaint statement.[1] We can enter its claim by noticing the quite different rhetorical moves made by the speaker.

1. The speaker is turned in on self in pity and self-preoccupation, and can speak of nothing but self (vv. 1–6):

> *I* cry aloud to God . . .
> *I* seek the Lord

1. See Brueggemann, *Praying the Psalms*, 8–11; Brueggemann, *Spirituality of the Psalms*, 25–45.

> *my hand* is stretched out,
>> *my soul* refuses to be comforted.
> *I* think of God,
> *I* moan
> *I* meditate,
>> *my spirit* faints,
>> *my eyelids* are kept by God from closing
> *I* am so troubled that *I* cannot speak
> *I* consider the days of old,
> *I* remember the years of long ago,
> *I* commune with *my heart*[2]
> *I* meditate and search *my spirit.*

The speaker does a complete inventory of his/her own person and sees how it is all, in every part, mobilized for self-concern.[3]

2. Then in vv. 7–9, there is a series of rhetorical questions. But even here there is no yielding of the agenda of self:

> Will the Lord spurn forever
>> and never again be favorable?
> Has steadfast love forever ceased?
>> Are his promises at an end for all time?
> Has God forgotten to be gracious?
>> Has he in anger shut up his compassion?

There is obviously a reference to Yahweh, more than appeared in vv. 1–6. But the rhetorical effort is to draw Yahweh completely into the orbit of self-concern. In these verses there occur three of Israel's most precious covenantal words, *chesed, chanan, racham*—loyalty, graciousness, compassion. The questions pose the most urgent faith issues. They ask about the very character of God. But they are questions that emerge out of an overriding self-concern.

---

2. "I commune with my heart" is a statement of religion reduced to self-preoccupation, not unlike the characterization of the Pharisee (John 18:11) who "prayed with himself."

3. The self-inventory is paralleled to the lamentation of Ps 22:17: "I count all my bones."

They appear to ask about God's faithfulness. But they really ask, *What about me?* Even the most primal qualities of Yahweh are consumed in this self-preoccupation. Thus far we are at the pool of Narcissus.[4] The speaker sounds as one who understands how it all works. He knows what mobilizes God's *chesed* and *racham*. She knows how to get to it. The crisis of the poem may be one of two things. Either the speaker knows how to make it all work, which means everything has been emptied of mystery; or, more likely, even though the speaker knows how to make it work, it does not work! It is then a religion that has failed.

Janzen has suggested that some rhetorical questions in the speech of the Old Testament are not mere rhetoric, but are serious questions.[5] Such questions ask the unaskable. In the form of a question the speaker moves into dangerous and unexplored territory in the space between us and the throne. In our psalm the speaker is a person of conventional obedience. He has some ground to stand on and some legitimate expectations of Yahweh. He is not a renegade who has forfeited his expectations from God. But the voice of obedience is on the move, driven there by the failure of convention. Her imagination is beginning to move, beginning to guess that God's *chesed* is not unilaterally unconditional and automatically linked to this particular believer. The poem begins to suspect that God's *chesed* (if indeed God is faithful!) has other worlds to work and cannot be summoned on demand. God is not on call. There is a probe here that the space between the two partners is dangerous and unknown space. All of that space has not yet been reduced and routinized so that it can be presumed upon. Some of the space between here and God's throne is untamed, and therefore unpredictable. And if the space is beyond

4. Lasch has made important linkages between the myth and the pathology of our time (*Culture of Narcissism*). One of the important ingredients in such immobilizing narcissism is the flattening of imagination so that the person is incapable of thinking of life other than it presently is, or incapable of thinking of life beyond self.

5. Janzen, "Metaphor and Reality in Hosea 11."

control, it makes one more frantically press for the old, innocent faith that had God encapsulated.

This speaker had grown comfortable with the great affirmations of Yahweh, because the great affirmations readily translated into self-serving assurance. But now that is all being blown out of the water. A God who has been reduced to the safe proposals of "a torah so righteous" (cf. Deut 4:8) now is known to be a God whose "form is not seen" (cf. Deut 4:12), even if that form is thought to consist in *chesed, chanan, racham*. The desperate rhetorical questions appear in vv. 7–9 after this self-inventory of vv. 1–6. The speaker begins to guess that the old sure religion is collapsing.

New Questions

There is a striking move from the "I, I, I," in vv. 1–6, which is still safely rooted and conventional and with no failure of nerve, to the probe of the questions of vv. 7–9, which ask new questions. And then there is v. 10. This verse is the crucial turn in the Psalm, exceedingly difficult to translate. This verse clearly looks both ways, back to the "I" statements of vv. 1–6, and forward to the rest of the psalm (vv. 11–20). It consists in two elements. The first element is a statement about *grief or trouble*.[6] The second element is a statement of *change*, presumably that God has changed. The translation is difficult, and there is some variation of nuance. RSV renders:

> It is my grief
> > that the right hand of the Most High has changed.

The Jerusalem Bible renders:

---

6. Calvin, *Commentary on the Book of Psalms II*, 214–15, takes the word from *hlh*, and understands it as "kill," (pierce) and renders it "my death." See the helpful and lucid comment of Anderson, *Book of Psalms*, vol. 2, 558.

"This" I said then "is what distresses me;
    that the power of the Most High is no longer what it was."

More poignantly, the New English Bible renders:

Has his right hand, I said, lost its grasp?
Does it hang powerless, the arm of the Most High?

Kraus comments: "God's works and ways are for human beings out of reach (Isa. 55:8ff.); they lie in an inaccessible, consuming brightness. He himself, Yahweh, is the Holy One (Pss. 71:22, 89:19), the 'wholly Other.' His salvific deeds prove his incomparability (cf. Exod. 15:11)."[7]

The speaker has discovered that Yahweh has freedom, will not be on call, not presumed upon. God is not locked into a *quid pro quo*. And it causes grief, illness, despondency to discern that the partner has changed. Observance of the freedom God has to change causes a terrible unsettling among the faithful. The sure comfort of an utterly obedient relationship is shattered by the awareness that this hidden, free God will not be fully discerned or completely predictable. And the response must be to break out of obedience of a simple kind for the practice of an imagination that seeks to find other ways of relating to this free God. To relate to such a free God requires freedom on the part of the believer, a freedom likely censored by the conventional religion of vv. 1–6.

The grief here expressed is not unlike the pouting of Jonah over God's graciousness (Jonah 4:1, 9). Only here the depression is more intense. And the substance moves in the opposite direction from that of Jonah. Jonah is disconcerted that God is gracious when he does not want God to be gracious. Here the psalmist is dismayed that God is not gracious when he had fully counted on that predictable graciousness.

The discernment of v. 10, anguished as it is, admits of more than one reading. If one is linked to a fiat one-dimensional faith, then this verse is *a bitter loss of faith*. But if we think in terms

7. Kraus, *Psalms 60–150*, 116.

of obedience on its way to risky imagination, then this verse is *an opening for new faith* beyond the conventions and routines that secure but do not reckon with God's awefulness. This verse stands at a very risky and dangerous place where evangelical faith often stands. And indeed must stand. And as we stand there, we never know in advance if we face *loss of faith* or *opening for new faith*. The dramatic substance of v. 10 leaves the issue quite unresolved. And we must not rush past that dramatic moment in this speech-pilgrimage.

A Wounded Partner

So the psalm makes its desperate way beyond v. 10. We have now the speech of a wounded partner well beyond the old innocence. We do not know how this speaker moves from v. 10 to v. 11. But we can surmise it was not an easy move. We do not know how any faith-speaker makes the leap from the preoccupation with self to an imaginative acknowledgment of the primacy of the other. But that is what happens in this Psalm and in all serious biblical faith. It involves leaving the safety of "the torah so righteous" for "the God so near" who is yet so free (Deut 4:7–8). The dramatic move concerns the abandonment of self as the primal agenda for the Thou who is out beyond us in freedom. And we make no mistake to observe that that transfer of the agenda, that ceding of concern for self to the other is the crucial move of biblical faith, the *sine qua non* for covenanting. And we observe what an urgent, difficult task Christian nurture and preaching now is. For the narcissism of our culture (on which see vv. 1–6) is precisely aimed at *not* ceding self, not relinquishing. This psalm models the very move of faith that our cultural ideology wants to prevent. The whole consumer perspective concerns retention of self and satiation of self. That is what is given in vv. 1–6 and what is relinquished in what follows.

Note that this was not the only move possible after v. 10. It is one among some options. After the wonderment of the questions of vv. 7–9 and the startling discovery of v. 10, another move could have been made. The speaker could have moved to Psalm 14 and concluded, "There is no God." The move beyond v. 10 is a hazardous one, for any of us. And the outcome is never sure ahead of time. But the move has been made here, a move that now reckons the free "Thou" as the starting point for life.[8]

That move, one of several possibilities, concerns us directly as we seek to be faithful and as we seek to live in our culture. On the one hand that move made in v. 11 is a move from a religion of law to a religion of grace. It articulates the awareness that we live by gift and not by grasp. On the other hand, observe that in our society of consumer narcissism, a *religion of petty moralistic obedience* goes with an *economics of satiation*. That is, in our secularized version of it, we do not hope for God to satisfy all our desires (Ps 145:16). But we do expect to have all our desires satisfied, even if by another source. So we are part of a culture that holds together *consumer satiation* and *petty obedience*. That tight alliance serves to keep *us* as the agenda, an excuse for not ceding life beyond self, an inability to transfer attention beyond our needs and appetites.

The religious temptation among us is to walk close to the dangerous rhetorical questions of vv. 7–9 and to become aware of the hurt and anguish of v. 10. But then not to move on to v. 11, not to move to the "Thou," but to circle back again to vv. 1–6, which permits a preoccupation with self (and self's program) and

---

8. Worth noting is the argument made here in sharp distinction from that of Gordon Kaufman in his excellent book, *Theological Imagination*, 63–75. If I read Kaufman correctly, he argues that the self-conscious assertion of "I" leads to the liberating reality of "Thou." I believe this psalm argues that the move is not from a full act of self-consciousness, but from relinquishment of self, precisely what modernity finds so difficult.

requires a numbing.[9] Because being numb will do, if there is no deliverance.

A New World of Imagination

By the mercy of God, the psalm does not circle back. And if it did, it would then be only a mirror for our fearful self-preoccupation. It would then not be a model of faith, but only an exercise in self-serving. But it moves on. It says something new and surprising and unpredictable. And that is why we attend to it. It moves on in remarkable fashion, so that v. 11 follows closely after v. 10. We may be glad for that modeling of the move. But we recognize at the same time that we do not know how it is possible. We presume that this move, here or anywhere, is not made easily or quickly. Likely there is a long pause in the psalm, a desperate resistance, a counting the cost, like standing at the edge of the cold swimming pool, testing it with a toe, putting it off, and then the quantum leap into the new icy world of imaginative faith. It is indeed a turning loose of the old self.

The move from vv. 1–10 to v. 11 is like the move envisioned by Jesus:

> For whoever would save his life will lose it;
>> and whoever loses his life for my sake and the gospel's will save it. (Mark 8:35)

The first part, with the series of "I," is about *keeping life.* And the move to the second part with the series of "Thou" is a readiness to *lose life in order to gain it.* I do not suggest that prayer and liturgy are the full scope of self-surrender. But I am very sure that unless there are liturgic ways for that move in our lives, we will not make them elsewhere, either with reference to personal maturation or

---

9. On "numbing" as the problem of our culture, see Soelle, *Suffering*; and especially the important work of Robert J. Lifton, whose major summary is *The Broken Connection.*

to social change. The very rhetoric of Israel here makes such a move thinkable, i.e., capable of being imagined.

There is a waiting, a hoping, a resisting, a yielding, a dying, a being surprised. By v. 11, the speaker has abandoned the pre-occupation with self and is able to focus on this one who "has changed," the same change that caused resentment and loss in v. 10.

1. By v. 11, the speaker is on the way into a new world of imagination. In vv. 1–6, the speaker had focused narrowly on "my present," which is all consuming. Now there is a reentry into "our past," which had been bracketed out in self-preoccupation. And in the pondering of that past, the speaker comes to the fresh awareness that it is precisely God's freedom to change and come and go that is the hope of Israel and the deliverance of folks like the speaker, in this present, or in any present.

In the second part of the psalm, a very different vocabulary is now at work:

v. 11	"deed" (*ma'alele*)
	"wonders" (*pil'ekah*)
v. 12	"work" (*pa'alekah*)
	"deeds" (*'alilothikah*)

These four terms are stated in a concise chiasmus. The key point is made in v. 13: "Thy way, O God, is holy (*qadosh*)." God's way is *ganz Anders* (wholly Other), not to be reduced, not to be accommodated or conformed either to my needs or my expectations. And then, following naturally, there is an assertion of incomparability: "What god is great like our God?" The question sounds like that of Deut 4:8 to which we have made reference. No god like ours, no god so near, no god so free, no god so surprising or exasperating. Here is the end to all analogy. And the bold, liberated speaker of vv. 11–20, discovers that the self-preoccupied speaker of vv. 1–6 was complaining about an idol, for this free God of *chesed, chanan, racham* will not be treated like a fortune cookie.

2. The remainder of the Psalm (vv. 15–20) is like a credo that recites the great deeds of the past. Verse 15 uses Exodus language with the verb *ga'al*. Verses 16–18 talk about a storm. It could be any storm god. The language is not unlike the Canaanite imagery of Psalm 29. But the language of the storm is regularly drawn toward this people. Verse 16 has echoes of Ps 114:3–4, which uses sea imagery for Exodus. Verses 17–18 are about a storm. But the point is for Israel in vv. 19–20, which becomes completely concrete and completely Israelite at the end, with the mention of Moses and Aaron.

Most striking about this psalm is its abrupt ending. Nothing here about a return to the agenda of vv. 1–6. There is nothing about all of that being resolved. It is as though the speaker is left to draw her own conclusions about the condition of vv. 1–6 in relation to the statements of vv. 15–20. Nothing has been resolved, but everything has been recontextualized. The speaker in vv. 1–6 is preoccupied because he is caught in a narrow range in which such personal trouble requires a conclusion that God does not care. That narrow religious agenda is, however, shattered. It is shattered by remembering, by awareness of God's incomparability, by reference to Israel's concrete history, but most of all it is shattered by the utterance, *Thou* (*'attah*).

Now I have dealt with this psalm in detail because I take it to be structurally the story of God's people who are always *trapped* and/or *on the move*. This Psalm knows that all of us live in this battle. We struggle to stay home with the sure company of "I." We move between a petty religion of calculating obedience aimed at well-being, and a fully liberated imaginative religion of awe and amazement and trembling before the Holy One. In this psalm, vv. 1–6 (7–9) articulate the first; vv. 11–20 speak about the alternative. The first is dominated by "I." The second is governed by "Thou."

> *Thou* art God (v. 14)
> *Thou* didst redeem thy people with *thine* own arm (v. 15)

the waters saw *thee*
the crash of *thy* thunder
   thy lightnings
   thy way was through the sea
 thy path through the great waters
    thy footprints unseen (vv. 18–19).
 Thou didst lead thy people (v. 20).

Note that after v. 12, there is not a single "I." One can observe that there is a neat contrast between the "my" of the first half—my trouble, my hand, my spirit, my eyelids, my soul, my heart, my spirit—and the "thy" in the second half—thy thunder, thy lightening, thy way, thy path, thy footprints. The rhetorical change cannot be accidental. The contrast is total, decisive, and intentional. And the turn is in v. 10. Everything is up for grabs in v. 10, waiting for fresh resolution. It is the pastoral moment that could go either way. It is the evangelical moment in which the news may break. It is a moment of deciding: to live in the world where the Most High changes, or to retreat back into a world where "least high" keeps us at the center of things. It is the pastoral task to be present to that moment of terror, a moment that requires enormous imagination.

4

Cadences That Redescribe:
Speech among Exiles

EXILE, THAT IS, SOCIAL, cultural displacement, is not primarily geographical, but it is liturgical and symbolic.[1] This was the case with the Judeans in exile in the sixth century BCE, as it is in our Western culture presently. In defining exile, Alan Mintz writes: "The catastrophic element in events [of exile] is defined as the power to shatter the existing paradigms of meaning, especially as regards the bonds between God and the people of Israel."[2] In such a situation where "paradigms of meaning" are shattered, it is clear that exiles must pay careful and sustained attention to speech, because it requires inordinately disciplined and imaginative speech to move through the shattering to newly voiced meaning. Mintz suggests that in exile, the primal speakers (poets) attempt, "first to *represent the catastrophe* and then to *reconstruct, replace, or*

1. On my understanding of exile as a useful metaphor for the contemporary crisis of the U.S. church, see Brueggemann, "Disciplines of Readiness"; and Brueggemann, "Preaching to Exiles."

2. Mintz, *Hurban: Responses to Catastrophe in Hebrew Literature*, x. I am indebted to Tod Linafelt for this most remarkable reference.

redraw the threatened paradigm of meaning, and thereby make creative survival possible."[3]

I find Paul Ricoeur's phrasing a useful way to understand what is required and what is possible for speech in such situations. Ricoeur speaks in terms of "limit experiences" that permit and require "limit expressions."[4] "Limit experiences" are those in which all conventional descriptions and explanations are inadequate. When one is pushed experientially to such extremity, one cannot continue to mouth commonplaces, but is required to utter something "odd."[5] The "odd" "limit expression" is in language that effectively "redescribes" reality away from and apart from all usual assumptions about reality.[6] Thus such speech invites the speaker and the listener into a world that neither had known before this utterance.

It is clear that in exile, while something utterly new must be uttered, that is, not contained within or regulated by past utterance, this daring speech that evokes newness nonetheless employs in fresh ways speech that is already known and trusted. In order to serve as "redescription," however, the already trusted speech must be uttered in daring, venturesome ways that intensify, subvert, and amaze.

By utilizing the theme of exile as an analogue by which to describe (redescribe?) our current social situation in the West, I suggest that our loss of the white, male, Western, colonial hegemony, which is deeply displacing for us, is indeed a "limit experience," whereby we are pushed to the edge of our explanatory and coping powers. Such experience requires "limit expression." Such a consideration belongs in a *Journal for Preachers*, precisely because preachers in such a "limit experience" have obligation

---

3. Ibid., 2.

4. Ricoeur, "Biblical Hermeneutics."

5. The "odd speech" with which Ricoeur deals includes proclamatory sayings, proverbs, and parables. Cf. ibid., 109–18.

6. Ibid., 127, and passim.

and possibility of being the very ones who can give utterance both to "represent the catastrophe" and to "reconstruct, replace or redraw" the paradigms of meaning that will permit "creative survival." I suggest that the preaching task now is nothing less than that twofold task.

In what follows I will consider four examples of "limit expression" that were utilized in that ancient exile of sixth century Judeans, in order that their "limit experience" of displacement could be embraced and moved through. My thought is that there are clues here for our own speech practice in a time of acute displacement and bewilderment.

Lamentation and Complaint

The first task among exiles is to *"represent the catastrophe"*: to state what is happening by way of loss in vivid images so that the loss can be named by its right name and so that it can be publicly faced in the depth of its negativity. Such naming and facing permits the loss to be addressed to God, who is implicated in the loss as less than faithful in a context seen to be one of fickleness and failure. Such speech requires enough candor to dare to utter the torrent of sensitivities that cluster, such as pain, loss, grief, shame, and rage. For this, of course, this ancient Jewish community found its best speech by appeal to the liturgic tradition of *lamentation* (which expresses sadness) and *complaint* (which expresses indignation).[7]

The richest, most extreme statement of sadness, punctuated by loss, helplessness, and vulnerability, is the book of Lamentations.[8] It is not much studied or used among us, no doubt because it has seemed so remote from our cultural situation. If, however, we are now in a new situation of profound loss, as I have

7. The basic book on lamentation is Westermann, *Praise and Lament in the Psalms*.

8. Mintz, *Hurban*, 17–48, has the most suggestive discussion of the book of Lamentations known to me. The most reliable commentary is Hillers, *Lamentations*.

suggested, this poetry could be for us an important "speech resource." The little book of Lamentations consists in five extended poems of grief over the destruction of Jerusalem (for which I have suggested as an analogue the loss of our accustomed privilege and certitude). In the first poem (chapter 1), the bereft city of Jerusalem is "like a widow," abandoned, shamed, vulnerable, subject to abuse, without an advocate or defender (1:1). The recurring theme of the abandonment of Jerusalem is expressed as "no one to comfort her" (vv. 2, 9, 16, 17); "no resting place" (v. 3); "no pasture" (v. 6); "no one to help" (v. 7). The imagery is of a woman overwhelmed with tears, under assault, and subject to abuse.[9] While there is in 3:21–33 a powerful statement of hope and confidence, the collection of Lamentations ends with a sense of "forsakenness": "Why have you *forgotten* us completely? Why have you *forsaken* us these many days?" (5:20).

This same sense of being "forgotten" is evident in the more abrasive and indignant complaint of Psalm 74. The poet is more aggressive in here describing to God the situation of dismay, and in pressing God to act.[10] The poem provides for God a play-by-

9. Mintz, *Hurban*, 24, most helpfully discerns what is at stake in this particular imagery:

> The serviceableness of the image of Jerusalem as an abandoned fallen woman lies in the precise register of pain it articulates. An image of death would have purveyed the false comfort of finality; the dead have finished with suffering and their agony can be evoked only in retrospect. The raped and defiled woman who survives, on the other hand, is a living witness to a pain that knows no release. It is similarly the perpetualness of her situation that comes through most forcefully when Zion is pictured as a woman crying bitterly alone in the night with tears wetting her face (1:2). The cry seems to ululate permanently in the night; the tear forever falls to the cheek. It is a matter not just of lingering suffering but of continuing exposure to victimization.

10. The contrast between the book of Lamentations and Psalm 74 is the difference between "lament" and "complaint." Gerstenberger, "Jeremiah's Complaints," 405 n. 50, draws the distinction nicely: "A lament bemoans a tragedy which cannot be reversed, while a complaint entreats God for help in the midst of tribulation." The distinction and interrelatedness of the two are nicely expressed in German, *Klage* and *Anklage*.

play of what "your foes" have done to "your holy place" (74:4; cf. vv. 4–9). It then moves to a doxology (see below), recalling to God God's own powerful miracles of the past (vv. 12–17). These concern God's sovereign rule over all of creation, and God's capacity to bring life out of chaos. By juxtaposing the present calamity of the temple and God's glorious past, the poem makes intercession that God should now act, both to defeat the impious enemies and to act so that "the downtrodden are not put to shame" (v. 21; cf. vv. 18–23). One is struck in this psalm with the directness of speech, the candor about the current trouble that is catastrophic, and the vigor with which God is expected to act in fidelity.

Through both the lamentation and the psalm of complaint, the catastrophic is vividly "represented," to make it palpable to God as it is to the community. My suggestion, insofar as our current Western dismay is a parallel to this ancient travesty, is that a primary pastoral task is to voice the felt loss, indignation, and bewilderment that are among us. The reason extreme imagery is required is that the speech must cut through the enormous self-deception of political-economic euphemism. For the truth is that the old, settled advantage in the world upon which we have counted is over and gone, as over and gone as was Jerusalem's temple. Sadness, pain, and indignation are not inappropriate responses to the loss, either then or now. They require abrasive, insistent speech to be available, and ancient Israel gives us a script for our own daring "representation" of the trouble.

Assurance

In the laments and complaints, Israel speaks to God. Israel takes the initiative in rightly naming its displacement to God. In times of debilitating dismay, it is the one who experiences the dismay who must courageously come to speech.[11] This is abundantly clear

---

11. On the cruciality of coming to speech, see Scarry, *The Body in Pain*; and Herman, *Trauma and Recovery*.

in the speech of ancient Israel. But Israel's "limit expressions" are not restricted to the voice of Israel. The voice of Yahweh also sounds in the daring rhetoric of the exile, precisely in the context where Israel had sensed its abandonment by God. Indeed, in the poetry of Deutero-Isaiah, God acknowledges that God has been silent too long and will now break that silence in powerful speech. God says, "For a long time I have held my peace, I have kept still and restrained myself; Now I will cry out like a woman in labor, I will gasp and pant" (Isa 42:14; cf. 62:1).[12] In the "salvation oracles" of Deutero-Isaiah, Israel hears the classic assurance that God is present with and for Israel, even in its dismay and displacement. Most precisely and succinctly, this oracle of assurance asserts on God's lips, "Fear not, for I am with you" (cf. Isa 41:13, 14; 43:1–5; 44:8; Jer 30:10–11).[13] Joseph Sittler among others has seen that this speech is closely paralleled to the way a parent reassures a child who has had a nightmare.[14] Such parental assurance is indeed a "redescription." Indeed, this assurance is a nightmare-ending speech, for it asserts a caring presence that is trusted enough and powerful enough to override the sense of absence evoked by the exile. Now, in this utterance, what had seemed to be a place of absence is known to be a place of presence, thereby invested with great potential for life.

While the salvation oracle proper is highly stylized, Claus Westermann has seen that there are great variations on the theme of assurance expressed in a variety of forms, including what he calls "assurance of salvation," "announcement of salvation," and "portrayal of salvation."[15] We do not need to pay too close attention to the variations in form. What counts for our consideration

12. There is a powerful play of imagery in the relation between Jerusalem as an abused widow and Yahweh as a restless woman about to give birth.

13. The most complete study of the genre is Conrad, *Fear Not Warrior*.

14. Sittler, *Grace and Gravity*, 99–100. See the more comprehensive discussion by O'Day, "Toward a Biblical Theology of Preaching."

15. Westermann, "The Way of the Promise through the Old Testament," 202–9.

is the situation-transforming capacity of the utterance, what Ricoeur would term "redescription."

Thus Lam 5:20 ends with a haunting sense of being "forgotten" and "forsaken": "Why have you *forgotten* us completely? Why have you *forsaken* us these many days?" In Isa 49:14, the same two terms are reiterated (probably deliberately quoted):

> But Zion said,
> "Yahweh *has forsaken* me,
> my Lord *has forgotten* me."

But then in 49:15–16, these haunting fearful questions are answered by the God who does not forget or abandon:

> Can a woman *forget* her nursing child,
> or show no compassion for the child of her womb?
> Even these may *forget*,
> yet I will not *forget* you.
> See, I have inscribed you on the palms of my hands;
> your walls are continually before me.

Or in Isa 54:10, after conceding that there had been a brief abandonment of Israel by God (vv. 7–8), and after comparing the devastation of the exile to the flood in Genesis (v. 9), the poet has God utter a sweeping assurance of God's reliable durability:[16]

> For the mountains may depart and the hills be removed,
> but my *steadfast love* shall not depart from you,
> and my *covenant of peace* shall not be removed,
> says Yahweh, who has *compassion* on you. (v. 10)

This triad of Yahweh's characteristics—steadfast love, covenant of peace, compassion—is more than enough to override the flood, to overcome the absence and shame, and to overmatch the terror of exile.

---

16. On this text, see Brueggemann, "A Shattered Transcendence? Exile and Restoration."

We are so familiar with such assurances that we may fail to notice what a daring act of faith such an utterance is, how blatantly it speaks against and beyond perceived circumstance in order to "reconstruct, replace, or redraw the threatened paradigm of meaning." It is an act of powerful faith on the part of the speaker, but also on the part of the listener. The intent of the assurance is to create faith in the listener. The exile was widely seen to be a season of God's absence, and now this poet dares to assert that God is present in that very circumstance, faithfully at work to bring a newness out of the defeat.

The analogue in our own time is for the preacher-poet of the gospel to make such an utterance in the midst of our failed privilege and hegemony. The utterance of assurance is not to prop up the old paradigm, for the assurance comes only after the "representation of the catastrophe," that is, after the felt and expressed situation of lamentation and complaint. The assurance asserts that in the very midst of economic displacement and bewilderment about sexuality, where all old certitudes are in profound jeopardy, just these meanings of a new kind are being wrought by the power and fidelity of God, "new things" shaped like covenantal faithfulness that will become visible only in, with, and through the displacement.[17] Such utterances are indeed "by faith alone." But then, that is always how the gospel is uttered in such problematic circumstance.

Doxologies of Defiance

The counterpole to lamentation and complaint is the hymn of praise, which emerges from "victory songs." That is, hymns are sung when situations of great trouble are transformed by the power and mercy of God. Israel has been singing such songs

17. I name economics and sexuality because these are the twin issues that vex and will continue to vex the church. It will be helpful to see that the two are deeply interrelated, as the parallel criticisms of Marx and Freud make clear.

since the deliverance from Egypt (Exod 15:1–18, 21). These daring doxologies sing what Israel has seen and heard about the decisive power and reliable commitment of Yahweh to intrude in life-giving ways in circumstances of defeat, disorder, and death. Thus the doxology of remembrance in Ps 74:12–17 reaches all the way back to creation and to God's capacity to order chaos. And the despondent worshipper in Ps 77:11–20 ponders the remembered Exodus. Out of these treasured, concrete memories, Israel's hymns also constitute acts of hope, confident that what God has done in the past is what God will do in the present and in the future.

In the exile, the doxologies are not primarily acts of remembering God's past "wonders," but they are anticipatory assertions concerning what God is about to do. Israel is summoned to sing a "new song," to sing praise for God's sovereign liberating action that is now about to occur (Isa 42:10).

In the situation of exile in Babylon, it was "self-evident" that the Babylonian gods had triumphed, that Yahweh had failed, either because of weakness or because of indifference. Either way, the evidence suggested that loyalty to Yahweh no longer worked or was worth practicing, because other powers could give more reliable and immediate payoffs.

The poetry of Deutero-Isaiah, however, will not accept that "self-evident" reading of reality. The hymns offered by the poet are assertions against the evident, insisting that Yahweh's saving power is at the break of new activity. Thus, Israel has concluded that God does not care about Israel:

> Why do you say, O Jacob,
>> and speak, O Israel,
> "My way is hidden from Yahweh,
>> and my right is disregarded by my God"? (Isa 40:27)

The responding hymn of vv. 28–31 asserts in wondrous lyric that Yahweh is the God of all generations, past, present, future, is not weary or faint or powerless, but gives power to those who hope. The outcome is not only a statement about God, but an assurance to those who trust this God:

> Those who wait for Yahweh shall renew their strength,
>> they shall mount up with wings like eagles,
> they shall run and not be weary,
>> they shall walk and not faint. (vv. 30–31)

Notice that the doxology completely rejects the notion of the rule of the Babylonian gods. Against their apparent rule, it is, so the hymn asserts, in fact Yahweh who holds power and who gives power (cf. Isa 46:1–4).

That same contrast is evident in the defiant doxology of Isa 41:21–29. Negatively the gods of Babylon are called to give account of themselves, and they fail miserably (vv. 21–23). This leads to the conclusion that they are nothing, nothing at all. Moreover, those who trust such "nothing gods" are as "nothing" as their gods.

> You, indeed, are nothing
>> and your work is nothing at all;
>> whoever chooses you is an abomination. (v. 24)

Positively, it is Yahweh who is able to act visibly, decisively, and transformatively (vv. 25–27). Israel's doxologies are characteristically against the data, inviting Israel to live in a "redescribed world," in which meaning has been "reconstructed, replaced, or redrawn."

In our own situation, the hymnic act of praise has become largely innocuous. It happens often among us that praise is either escapist fantasy, or it is a bland affirmation of the status quo. In fact, doxology is a daring political, polemical act that serves to dismiss certain loyalties and to embrace and legitimate other loyalties, and other shapes of reality.[18]

18. See Brueggemann, "Praise and the Psalms: A Politics of Glad Abandonment."

In the context of Deutero-Isaiah, the hymnic wager is on Yahweh's intention for homecoming, and therefore the refusal of the Babylonian gods who seek to define the world in noncovenantal ways. In our situation of upheaval and confusion, hymns that celebrate the God of the Bible wager on a covenantal-neighborly world powered by the neighborliness of God, and wager against any characterization of the world that bets on selfishness, greed, fear, abuse, or despair. Our current world of bewilderment is often described as though everything good is ending, as though the forces of chaos have won. This hymnic tradition authorizes the church to identify and redescribe this present place as the arena in which the rule of the creator-liberator God is working a wondrous newness. Our singing and utterance of such lyric faith assert that we will not submit to the gods of fear and anticovenantal power relations. In such a situation as ours, the words and music for a "new song" are acts of powerful renewal.

Promises

The assurances and hymns upon which we have commented are anticipatory. That is, they look to the resolve of Yahweh to work a newness that is not yet visible or in hand. Exiles, however, have a way of speech that is more directly and singularly preoccupied with God's sure future, namely, oracles of promise. Israel believes that God can indeed work a newness out of present shambles, and that that newness will more fully embody God's goodwill for the world. It is cause for amazement that Israel's most daring and definitional promises were uttered in exile, that is, precisely when the evidence seems to preclude such hope. The promises are assertions that God is not a prisoner of circumstance, but that God can call into existence that which does not exist (cf. Rom 4:17).

Here I will cite three of the best known and most powerful of such exilic promises. In Jer 31:31–34 the promise asserts that God will work a new covenant with Israel that is aimed at

Torah obedience (v. 33), but is rooted in the overriding reality of forgiveness (v. 34).[19] The dominant assumption about exile in the Old Testament, propounded especially in the Deuteronomic tradition, is that exile is punishment (2 Kgs 17:7-23; see even Isa 40:2). This promise, in the face of a theology of guilt-and-punishment, is an assertion that forgiveness will overpower sin, and Israel's primal theological reality is the future-creating graciousness of Yahweh who will "remember their sin no more."[20]

In Ezek 37:1-14, the prophet Ezekiel searches for an adequate metaphor for exile and homecoming. The most extreme imagery available is that exile equals death. But from death, there is no hope for the power of death is strong and decisive. In a radical rhetorical break, however, the prophet dares to assert that by the power of God's spirit, "I will open your graves," that is, "I will place you on your own soil" (vv. 13-14). Exile is not the last word, that is, death is not the last reality. Israel's situation is not hopeless, because God's transformative wind (spirit) blows even in the dismay of exile, in order to work a newness toward life.

The poem of Isa 65:17-65 (which may be dated slightly after the return from exile in 520 BCE) offers a "portrayal of salvation" in stunning anticipatory fashion. The poet anticipates a new earth and a new Jerusalem characterized by new social relations, new economic possibilities, and new communion with God. Indeed, the poet foresees a complete and concrete inversion of Israel's current situation of hopelessness.

Notice that all of the promises, specific as they are, are cast as God's own speech, the authority for which is not found in any visible circumstance, but in the trustworthiness of the God who speaks. It is God's own resolve to work a newness that will impinge upon what seems to be a closed, hopeless situation.

19. See the helpful discussion of this passage by Lohfink, *The Covenant Never Revoked*, 45-57. Lohfink makes clear that the text cannot be interpreted in a Christian, supersessionist way.

20. On "forgiveness," see especially the exilic text of 1 Kgs 8:27-53.

Exiles inevitably must reflect upon the power of promise, upon the capacity of God to work a newness against all circumstance.[21] Promise has become nearly an alien category among us. That is partly an intellectual problem for us, because our Enlightenment perception of reality does not believe that there can be any newness "from the outside" that can enter our fixed world. And partly the loss of promise is a function of our privilege in the world, whereby we do not in fact want newness, but only an enhancement and guarantee of our preferred present tense.

As our white, male, Western privilege comes to an end, we are likely to experience that "ending" as terrible loss that evokes fear and resentment.[22] Evangelical faith, however, dares to identify what is (for some) an alienating circumstance as the matrix for God's newness (for all). Thus evangelical speech functions to locate the hunches and hints and promises that seem impossible to us that God will indeed work in the midst of our frightening bewilderment. But the preacher will work primarily not from visible hints and hunches, precisely because hope is "the conviction of things not seen," a conviction rooted in the trusted character of God.

The Ministry of Language

Speech, or as Mintz terms it, "the ministry of language," is one of the few available resources for exile.[23] Exiles are characteristically stripped of all else, except speech. And what exiles do is to speak

21. On the practice of promise among exiles in order to fight off despair, see Alves, *Tomorrow's Child*, 182–205. Alves writes: "Why is it so important to go on hoping? Because without hope one will be either dissolved in the existing state of things or devoured by insanity," 193.

22. My use of the term "end" here as a sense of terrible loss is intended to counter the argument of Fukuyama, *The End of History and the Last Man*. In my judgment his self-serving argument, i.e., self-serving for Western capitalism, is a romantic fantasy. He understands the current "end" to be one of triumph.

23. Mintz, *Hurban*, 29.

their "mother tongue," that is, the speech learned as children from mother, as a way to maintain identity in a situation that is identity-denying.

In that ancient world of displacement, the Judeans treasured speech that was "redescriptive," precisely because it was not derived from or sanctioned by the managers of the exile. It was, rather, derived from older speech practice of the covenanted community, and sanctioned by the evangelical *chutzpah* of poets who dared to credit such defiant utterances as complaints and lamentations, assurances, hymns, and promises. These are indeed forms of speech from Israel's "mother tongue."

In the "modernist" church of our time (liberal and conservative), there has been a loss of "mother-speech," partly because of subtle epistemological erosion, and partly because we imagine that other forms of speech are more credible and "make more sense." The truth is, however, that speech other than our own gradually results in the muteness of the church, for we have nothing left to say when we have no way left to say it. Exiles need, first of all and most of all, a place in which to practice liberated speech that does not want or receive the legitimacy of context. I take it that the old "paradigms of meaning" are indeed deeply under threat among us. We can scarcely pretend otherwise. We may learn from our ancestors in faith that in such a context, we must indeed "represent the catastrophe" and then "reconstruct, replace, or redraw" the paradigms of meaning. Both tasks are demanding. It belongs nonetheless to the speakers rooted in this tradition of liberated, defiant, anticipatory speech to take up these tasks. It is in, with, and from such speech that there comes "all things new."

5

The Secret of Survival

JEREMIAH DECLARES THAT "THIS people" and "this city" are like a broken pot that cannot be mended (Jeremiah 19). When he announced this devastating verdict upon the Jerusalem establishment, he predictably evoked harsh response. In Jeremiah 20, Pashur, a high sacral bureaucrat who in this chapter enjoys his fifteen minutes of fame, arrested Jeremiah as an enemy of the state. He punished him by putting him in stocks "in the Upper Benjamin Gate" of the temple. This caused Jeremiah in turn to unleash a strong invective against the official and against all Judah, all the wealth of the city, all its profits, all its prized belongings, and all its treasures. He asserted that all was under immediate threat by the harsh judgment of God.

That abrasive exchange brings us to our text in chapter 20. I settled on this sequence because in the company of pastors and priests—it could be any of us—we all know about saying a word and being labeled an enemy of all that is treasured, if not arrested then isolated, if not publicly scored, then at least a subject of many monstrous rumors, much gossip, and cancelled pledges. And all because one is boldly faithful, reasonably faithful in the service of one's call, but perceived by others as an enemy of all that is precious.

This sermon is only for those among us who find yourselves in conflict, under assault, in deep tension for the practice of faith. It is for you, even if you have not been publicly humiliated with stocks in the public square. But it is only for those few among us in such dispute. Others of you may listen or leave, but it is not for you.

The narrative sequence of prophetic declaration, arrest, and invective intensified the dispute in Jerusalem and caused the zealous prophet to sink into deep turmoil and doubt, leaving us with questions: What should happen next in the text? What word should come next in the text? Well, the editors of the book of Jeremiah have decided what comes next, and it strikes me as a good decision. After the harsh public exchange, the break from the narrative in 20:6 to the poem in 20:7 is an abrupt move from public dispute to Jeremiah at prayer. It is in prayer that this man of deep dispute finds sustenance for his life and his ministry; he finds sustenance, however, only by continued dispute, this time in secret. Only this time it is dispute with the God who has called him into this unbearable ministry in the first place.

I have always read Jesus' injunction to us in the Sermon on the Mount as an imperative to privacy, in order to avoid high phrases and ostentatious spirituality. Maybe that is what Jesus intends. He said, as you know:

> But whenever you pray,
> > go into your room and shut the door
> > and pray to your Father who is in secret;
> > > and your Father who sees in secret will reward you.
> When you are praying,
> > do not heap up empty phrases as the Gentiles do,
> > > for they think that they will be heard because of
> > > their many words.
>
> (Matt 6:6–7)

When the teaching of Jesus on prayer is connected to the crisis of Jeremiah, however, a different thought occurs to me. Maybe the reason for prayer in secret, rather than the danger of public display, is that Jeremiah is about to get down and dirty with the God who calls him. Jeremiah must pray in secret, not because to pray in public is a temptation to ostentatiousness as much as it is that such prayer in public would be a scandal to both prophet and God, for things must be said that are not for the curious, censorious ears of Pashur. Jesus says do it in secret: "Go to your room and shut the door and pray to your Father who is in secret; and your Father who sees in secret will reward you." This is the one from whom no secret can be hid!

But the secret that cannot be hid from the Father is not that one has a big wish list to speak to the hearer of our prayers. Nor is the secret that Jeremiah has deep sins about which God already knows. Not petition and not confession, but simply the transaction of genuine, honest dialogue with no holds barred, a dialogue upon which life depends and upon which ministry must be premised. I propose that it is this secret exchange with no holds barred that is the secret of survival for this Jeremiah whose very survival is at risk because of the accusatory onslaught of the establishment. My thought in this sermon is a simple one: the public ministry of Jeremiah in 20:1–6 (including his arrest and humiliation) is juxtaposed to the prayer of 20:7–13 because it is *secret prayer* that permits energy, freedom, and courage for *public ministry*.

The servants who faithfully show God to the world are those who live in deep, disputatious conversation with God. I think this is worth talking about because I believe faithful ministry in time to come will be increasingly a contested practice that will test our faith and require both every resource we can muster and every resource that God will give us. The ultimate resource for ministry, I propose, is honest conversation with God through which God is drawn, deep and thick, into the needfulness of our ministry. So consider this prayer that rendered Jeremiah bold and fearless in public places.

The prayer begins in truth-telling against God, *a bold accusation* that borders on paranoia:

> O Yahweh, you have enticed me,
>> and I was enticed;
> You have overpowered me,
>> and you have prevailed.
> I have become a laughing stock all day long;
>> everyone mocks me. (20:7)

Strong language this. The God who called the prophet is a trickster who has lured into vocation under false pretenses. Along with wile, this calling God has coerced and forced and left the prophet with no alternative. Jeremiah had protested against the call at the outset, but God would not be persuaded otherwise. As a result, Jeremiah is forced to become this voice that warns, accuses, exposes, and undermines in Jerusalem. He had said, in his vivid imagery, that his society is on the way to death by its foolish choices that lead to foolish, God-defying policies. That is all that he had said; but he had to say it.

The vocation is too hard. But it turns out that the prophet has only two choices:

> For whenever I speak, I must cry out,
>> I must shout, "Violence and derision!"
> For the word of Yahweh has become for me
>> a reproach and derision all day long.
> if I say, "I will not mention him,
>> or speak any more in his name,"
> then within me there is something like a burning fire
>> shut up in my bones.
> I am weary with holding it in,
>> and I cannot.
> for I hear many whispering:
>> "Terror is all around!

Denounce him! Let us denounce him!"
All my close friends are watching for me to stumble.
"Perhaps he can be enticed,
and we can prevail against him,
and take our revenge on him." (20:8–10)

Two choices: he can *speak*, and that leads to all kinds of hostil-
ity and alienation, rejection by close friends, rejection on every
side; or he can *be silent*, and then the stuff burns on the inside.
Either speech or silence. Either way unbearable, all because of the
seductive God of Israel who has forced him into an impossible
vocation. Better not to have been called; better not to notice or to
care. But now all those options are gone; the poet has run out of
options. The God who promised to support him is no support at
all; that God is fickle and now must listen to this assault of prayer
. . . all in secret, no holds barred, down and dirty. The prayer is in
secret, the text is unsuspected by his contemporaries, the inten-
sity is unrecognized, all necessary to survival, but in secret.

But then a reversal of sentiment. In public one must be
consistent, coherent, measured. In secret, however, one can be
as self-contradictory and herky-jerky as one's teeming, self-contradictory emotions require. This God accused is *the God to be
trusted*, because the prophet is innocent, has kept his call, and so
counts completely upon this harsh God to be ally and guardian:

But Yahweh is with me like a dread warrior;
therefore my persecutors will stumble,
and they will not prevail.
They will be greatly shamed,
for they will not succeed.
Their eternal dishonor
will never be forgotten.
O Yahweh of hosts, you test the righteous,
you see the heart and the mind:
Let me see your retribution upon them,
for to you I have committed my cause. (20:11–12)

This God is still ferocious, still powerful, still overriding; only now as Jeremiah's ally. This is the God who prevailed over Jeremiah. And now Jeremiah is utterly certain that none of his enemies can prevail, precisely because God is dread warrior who will withstand every onslaught. For a moment God was enemy, in that moment when all were enemy. But when Jeremiah remembers clearly that his enemy is Pashur, that sacral bureaucrat and the men of Anathoth, he is able to acknowledge God, in his desperate prayer, as a friend and ally.

God is trustworthy, strong, but not fickle. This is the very God to whom prayers can be reliably made, not a nice God, not a therapeutic God, not a warm fuzzy God, not a dear uncle, but God of hosts, God with hard capacities and stern resolves. Jeremiah prays to and trusts this God, because he himself cannot withstand his persecutors, and he will not appeal to a God who is kind but helpless.

So in secret he prays to this God,

who will do for him what he cannot do for himself,
who will prevail for him against every enemy threat,
who will remember the shame of the adversary,
who will work retaliation upon the enemy.

This *desperate man* has become this *confident man* through this secret negotiation in which the truth is told. Jeremiah had not needed to be polite or consistent, and now does not need to be modest or gentle. It is in secret and so he can move to the deepest extremity of confidence, a confidence adequate even for his desperate social context.

Accusation turns to *confidence*. And now in v. 13 *confidence* turns to glad, yielding *praise*:

Sing to Yahweh;
praise Yahweh!
For he has delivered the life of the needy
from the hands of the evildoers.

What a voice! Who would have thought in v. 7 that Jeremiah would get to that cadence of doxology! No doubt he is still surrounded by evildoers like Pashur who would like to put him permanently in stocks . . . or worse. No doubt he will soon have to go back into the fray, out beyond his closet of secret prayer, for that is his calling and he cannot duck it. He now does not want to duck it; he now knows that if he ducks it he will get acute heartburn "like a burning fire shut up in my bones." Still the same role, still the same adversaries, but new in God, now assured yet again that the God who calls is the God who delivers all the needy, but particularly delivers this needy prophet who has no other resource.

The dramatic turn in this verse is astonishing. How did Jeremiah make that move? Well, perhaps God came to him somewhere in the midst of this poem, reiterating the assurance, "I am with you." Such dramatic reentry by God, however, is only possible for the public prophet who practices a second, hidden life of faith. In that hidden life of faith, the prophet is not advocate, not shrill moralist, not cocksure about the great public issues, but rather is down and dirty, down and dirty enough to learn again that the God who calls and lures and avenges is not the God of social action or covenantal Torah or righteous indignation, but is the down and dirty God with whom talk must be daring, who must be assaulted and challenged and resisted and defied . . . and eventually praised. So this text and this sermon are for pastors for whom life is unbearable in stress and tension. The text is an assertion that for all the coping techniques of stress management and time management and support groups—all-important in themselves—that in the end the issue is an intimate theological one. There must be *deep freedom in secret* with the holy, calling God in order that there be *deep courage in public ministry*. Without such secret, the public practice becomes one of cynicism or accommodation or a dozen other forms of fickleness.

I must be honest enough to tell you that if you read past v. 13 into vv. 14–18, the prophet immediately falls out of doxology into what sounds like despair and depression. It would be better if doxology were the final word and the chapter ended in v. 13. But of course doxology never is the final word. After doxology there is always the deep reality of intransigence that talks us out of praise and into self-pity. Of course. That reality is known to every person called of this God.

Clearly, however, the depth of vv. 14–18 is also not final. Jeremiah moves past that as well. For he is soon back after that again into fierce confrontation about the truth that must be told. He moves past despair because he now has resources. He has the God who calls him, the promise of presence, and the chance to go back to v. 7 and say it all again, always again, and arriving always again at a moment of doxology. What we know in ministry is that we never arrive. We just stay at it and do it again. We do it again in public. But we do it in public because we do it in secret. We move back and forth. We survive . . . just barely . . . but we survive.

There was good reason for Jesus to say what he did about prayer. Prayer in public is too polite for those who find themselves in deep vocations. We may find the shrewdness of Jesus seconded by the poetic imagination of John Donne. He offers as a prayer:

> Batter my heart, three-personed God; for you
> As yet but knock, breathe, shine, and seek to mend;
> That I may rise and stand, o'erthrow mee, and bend
> Your force to break, blow, burn, and make me new.
> I, like an usurpt towne, to'another due,
> labor to'admit you, but Oh, to no end;
> Reason, your viceroy in mee, mee should defend,
> But is captive, and proves weak or untrue.
> yet dearly I love you and would be loved faine,
> But am betrothed unto your enemy.
> Divorce me, 'untie or break that knot again;
> Take mee to you, imprison mee, for I,
> Except you enthrall mee, never shall be free,
> Nor ever chaste, except you ravish mee. (Sonnet 14)

The very God who puts us in harm's way is the one to whom we turn in deepest intimacy, there in servitude to be set free, there to be healed, healed and imprisoned, drawn to rage and resentment, seeking for revenge, rising to praise, all moments of real life given us in secret with our secret enemy become the one who loves us most deeply and most dearly.

The news is that *survival* is *a secret art.* It depends upon renderings that are honest, conflicted, ragged, and lyrical. We are offered such a secret of survival, and then back to the public place. We go there on behalf of the God who promised at the outset:

> But you, gird up your loins; stand up and tell them everything that I command you. Do not break down before them, or I will break you before them. And I for my part have made you today a fortified city, an iron pillar, and a bronze wall, against the whole land—against the kings of Judah, its princes, its priests, and the people of the land. They will fight against you; but they shall not prevail against you, for I am with you, says Yahweh, to deliver you. (Jer 1:17–19)

Jeremiah can remember that initial assurance and prays it back to God confidence:

> But Yahweh is with me like a dread warrior;
>> therefore my persecutors will stumble,
>> and they will not prevail. (Jer 20:11)

Praise will not last, cannot last. But it is a treasured moment, a nervy assertion. Jeremiah gives thanks for life given again:

> Sing praise to Yahweh;
>> praise Yahweh!
> For he has delivered the life of the needy
>> from the hands of the evildoers. (Jer 20:13)

His prayer is part of the larger prayer of hope that the church and all its pastors sing in the face of evil:

The kingdom of the world has become the kingdom of our Lord
 and of his Messiah,
and he will reign forever and ever. (Rev 11:15)

Secret survival, public ministry, large hope, sure promise, and all
the while truth-telling . . . enough to keep going, again and again,
and going and going and going.

6

To Whom Does the Land Belong?

THE PRAGMATIC QUESTION CONCERNING creation is not evolution or "intelligent design." It is who owns, governs, and guarantees the earth; the question is made concrete and urgent when we remember that the biblical word "earth" (ʾerets) is most often translated "land." Thus the creation question is *Who has a right to the land?*

The Land Belongs to Yahweh

I begin with three biblical texts that ponder that issue: The most familiar verse to us is in the doxological beginning of Psalm 24: The earth is Yahweh's and all that is therein. *Yhwh ha-ʾarets.* I offer the Hebrew so that we may see that the earth/land is ʾerets and the owner is Yahweh, indicated by a possessive preposition. The land belongs to Yahweh! What follows in the psalm concerning this "king of glory" is an ethic that is congruent with the "owner" (vv. 3–6). The psalm concerns a ritual entry by Yahweh into the temple to enact and dramatize Yahweh's proprietorship of the land.

The same claim is made for Yahweh in Hosea 9 wherein the prophet anticipates that disobedient Israel will be expelled from "the land of Yahweh" and placed under control of hostile superpowers:

> They shall not remain in the land of Yahweh;
> > but Ephraim shall return to Egypt,
> > and in Assyria they shall eat unclean food. (Hos 9:3)

The Hebrew is *'erets Yhwh*. It is assumed that the land belongs to Yahweh and must therefore be organized and governed according to Yahweh's will and character. Israel has violated that will and therefore cannot remain as Yahweh's beloved people.

The question is put differently in 2 Sam 3:12, wherein Abner puts a defiant chiding rhetorical question to David: "To whom does the land belong" (*lemi-'erets*)? Again the land is *'erets* and again the possessive pronoun is the same as in Ps 24:1. Only here the issue from Abner to David is whether the land (the territory of north Israel) should be controlled by David or left to the remnant of Saul's enterprise. As the strongest of Saul's party, Abner is proposing to cede the land over to David—for a price. Thus Abner's question is a cynical one that appeals to David's rough and tumble notion of political advancement.

What strikes one most is that Abner (or the narrator) has completely forgotten the doxological liturgies of Israel that regularly acknowledge that the land belongs to Yahweh, the Creator. Abner reckons only that the land *belongs to David* or the land *belongs to Saul*. When the question is posed in that cynical way—as it most often is posed in "the real world"—the claim of Yahweh and the derivative claim of proper governance are readily and easily driven from the horizon. The calculating challenge of Abner to David is of interest and importance because the question of Abner—rather than a liturgical theology of creation—most often dictates political, economic, and military policy, and a self-serving sense of entitlement in the world. Thus I propose to consider *creation faith* around the urgent questions of ownership, control, and governance of the land and its embedded natural resources.[1]

Strength versus Vulnerability

When the Creator God is eliminated from the question of land/ creation, then the land question is characteristically resolved—as Abner assumed—on the basis of *power*, without any question about *legitimacy*. Thus in large scope it is fair to say that the story of ownership, control, and governance of the land is a narrative of *strength* against *vulnerability*:

The strong characteristically claim land and resources that belong to the weak;

the whites, since the fifteenth century, have claimed what belongs to other "races";

males have characteristically claimed what otherwise belongs to females;

Western nations, in the name of missionaries-cum-colonialism have claimed what has belonged to the non-West—or the non-North;

The developed powers with enormous technological advantage have claimed what "underdeveloped" powers cannot defend for themselves.

The story of the land is the story of power, confiscation, and usurpation that is rooted in a crass sense of entitlement. Wherever those who are able to enjoy the outcomes of shameless power, the claim is most often cast in well-sounding cadences of legitimacy.

---

1. J. Paul Getty once cynically remarked, "The meek shall inherit the earth, but that does not say anything about mineral rights under the earth."

Yahweh as Creator

Amid that enactment of *shameless power* with *cadences of legitimacy*, biblical faith asserts Yahweh as Creator, a claim that makes all human claims to the land to be penultimate. The church's confession of "Yahweh as Creator" (readily expressed in Trinitarian formulation so that all persons of the Trinity constitute the agency of creation) stands first in the Bible and first in the creeds. The church, in its confession of "God as Creator," asserts that the earth (land) is not an autonomous commodity, a freestanding entitlement; it is not, moreover, an available commodity to be taken in a crapshoot or to be divided by lots as was "his seamless garment" (Ps 22:18). It is rather a creature of Yahweh, well beloved and cared for by the Creator, blessed (Gen 1:22), looked over (Deut 11:12), and regularly renewed in generativity and fruitfulness.

Human utilization and human enjoyment of the land—the use of its resources—comes under the rubric of "love of God." Indeed the command to love God "with all your heart and with all your soul and with all your might" (Deut 6:5) is designed precisely for entry into the land:

> Now this is the commandment—the statutes and the ordinances—that Yahweh your God charged me to teach you to observe in the land that you are about to cross into and occupy, so that you and your children and your children's children may fear Yahweh your God all the days of your life, and keep all his decrees and his commandments that I am commanding you, so that your days may be long. Hear therefore, O Israel, and observe them diligently, so that it may go well with you, and so that you may multiply greatly in a land flowing with milk and honey, as Yahweh, the God of your ancestors, has promised you. (Deut 6:1–3)

Love of God correlates with occupation of land; consequently, *love of God* means to *order the land* in ways that are congruent with Yahweh's character; this character, we know everywhere in

Scripture, is marked by mercy, graciousness, steadfast love, compassion, fidelity, generosity, and forgiveness.

And of course if we characterize the proper ordering of land in such covenantal ways, it follows that the way we may "love God" in land-as-creation is to love neighbor, for finally we have no other way to love God (1 John 4:20–21). Thus our love of God is to order the land for the sake of the common good. We may then articulate dramatic lines of the land ethic in Scripture:

> the land belongs to Yahweh;
>
> the mandate is to love God in the land;
>
> we may love God in the land by loving neighbor.

The land, its potential for power, and its resources are to be devoted to the *common good*, that *all the neighbors* are to enjoy the fruitfulness and well-being of land as God's creation.

The Church's Forfeiture

That remarkable and central biblical claim about creation/land is the primary point of proclamation in the church that is rooted squarely in the creed. It is a most elemental claim of faith that now needs insistent voicing. But the church, in recent times, has largely forfeited its capacity for such proclamation. That forfeiture is on the one hand due to the church's endless and disproportionate preoccupation with "sin and salvation" of a privatistic kind; among the more sophisticated among us, on the other hand, the forfeiture is due to a commitment to "God's mighty deeds in history," as though God were known in dramatic events to the exclusion of the slow, steady, steadfast ordering of lived reality.[2]

The church's forfeiture of this crucial dimension of faith on both counts has left the issue of land outside the horizon of

---

2. It was Claus Westermann who first summoned Old Testament studies back to these issues by observing that the God who "saves" is the God who "blesses" (*What Does the Old Testament Say about God?*).

preaching, and has left our understanding of land in the categories of modern Enlightenment possessiveness.[3] For a time, we were all smitten with the famous article of Lynn White that claimed that the Genesis text on "dominion" was the root of land domination and exploitation in the world (Gen 1:28).[4] That connection, offered of course in "scientific" garb, has now been discredited and shown to be a careless and massive over-reading of the text. It is now clear that it is not the Bible but modern Enlightenment philosophy—rooted in Bacon, Descartes, and Locke—that in fact offered the modern Western world a notion of land as *absolute possession and property*.[5] Without the claim of a vigorous God articulated in political idiom, the land has been readily handed over to human possession and exploitation, whether under divine kings in the seventeenth century, nation states in the eighteenth century, military superpowers in the nineteenth and twentieth centuries, or simply enormous "McMansions" in gated communities in the twenty-first century. Once the claim of the Creator God has been sidelined, the sense of human entitlement may stretch in the contemporary world all the way from private consumer desires to aggressive imperial pursuit of oil as "our oil." The inevitable outcome is a loss of the common good, and a refusal to finance through taxes an infrastructure that will keep life livable, because taxes take away from private self-aggrandizing.

The preacher, so I suggest, is placed as a witness and advocate for *land as creation* in a society that is ideologically committed to *land as possession*. The preacher is summoned to a contestation that is enormously difficult, precisely because both private entitlement and national-corporate aggression are rooted in an ideology that remains unexposed and unrecognized, even though diametrically opposed to the church's creed concerning

3. See a classic statement by McPherson, *The Political Theory of Possessive Individualism*.

4. White, "The Historical Roots of Our Ecological Crisis."

5. See Wybrow, *The Bible, Baconism, and Mastery over Nature*. Wybrow has effectively answered the charges of White.

the Creator God and God's Christ in whom "all things hold together" (Col 1:17). Indeed this alien ideology holds that all things fall apart in the service of private good, and there is no category in that ideology for any common good, the very "good" that is the intent of the Creator.

Eminent Domain, Confiscation, Usurpation, Arrogant Autonomy

This ideology of private possession in denial of the Creator and at the expense of the neighbor has been given its classic expression in Enlightenment thought wherein the European intelligentsia managed to purge the claims of the biblical God from its horizon.[6] But the ideology itself is much, much older, even as it has reached virulent form in the contemporary world. Thus the ideology of private possession permeates the thinking of liberals and conservatives who have never heard of Bacon or Locke, relying rather on the declarations of Margaret Thatcher and the vigorous "innocence" of Ronald Reagan, imitated in haphazard and uncritical modes by George W. Bush. That ideology is pervasive, enhanced by the consumerism of the relentless liturgies of television.

As a consequence, when the preacher begins to talk about creation as God's ownership, control, and governance of the land, the preacher heads directly into a most deeply held and largely unrecognized and uncriticized alternative. The task of preaching, for that reason, is as urgent as it is risky. In what follows I will list four examples of that ideology and then cite three modest concrete signs of alternative around which the preacher may stake a claim. Here are four clear examples of the ideology of private possession against which creation faith makes its testimony, four ways in which to disturb creation and vex the Creator to whom the land belongs:

6. See the discussions of the theological crisis of the Enlightenment by Paul Hazard, *The European Mind*; and Stephen Toulmin, *Cosmopolis*.

1. The *exercise of eminent domain* whereby the powerful, with smart lawyers, seize the "inheritance" of the vulnerable. The narrative of 1 Kings 21 is a case study in such socioeconomic disruption. King Ahab wants the property of Naboth for a vegetable garden and promises Naboth appropriate compensation (v. 3). The narrative turns on the voiced vocabulary of Ahab and Nathan, terms that bespeak rival theories of economics and competing notions of land as creation. Ahab regards the land as a "possession," a commodity for buying and selling and trading—one piece of land is as good as another (v. 15). Naboth by contrast, speaks of "ancestral inheritance" to which he is intrinsically and inalienably attached (v. 3).[7] In this contest, the powerful, as usual, will prevail. In the land theory of Naboth, an old peasant presupposition, not only is ancestral land inviolate, but in fact pertains to the very ordering of creation.[8] It need hardly be added that the king's promise to compensation to Naboth was not forthcoming, even as a promised compensation for the exercise of eminent domain in the Atlanta Olympics in 1996 was not forthcoming. Those who regard land as a tradable commodity tend to have amnesia about long-term neighborly loyalty.

2. *Confiscation.* The narrative case I cite is in 2 Kgs 8:1–6. A woman, the one whose son had died who was raised to new life by Elisha (1 Kgs 4:8–37), had fled the land in the face of an acute famine. But of course the practice of confiscating economics did not cease in her absence. When she returned, she discovered she had lost "her house and her field" (v. 3). There is no suggestion that the loss was illegal or immoral, just the normal working of the economy.

---

7. Behind the notion of ancestral inheritance, as voiced by Naboth, is the large vision of the Jubilee. That provision makes no sense unless there is a commitment to protect ancestral property.

8. Reference may also be made to the narrative concerning Jeremiah's ancestral rootage in Jeremiah 32. That narrative in Jeremiah betokens the inalienable right of the exilic community to the land of Israel.

In her loss she "appealed" to the king. The verb is to "cry out," the desperate strategy of the vulnerable who announce in loud ways the suffering inflicted by the working of the powerful (see Luke 18:1–8). The woman addresses her appeal to the king who has the capacity to redress such confiscation and to return to her what is hers. We do not know why the king honored her appeal, as kings often do not. Perhaps this king, son of Ahab, had learned something by a study of the narrative of Naboth's vineyard; or perhaps he was under the influence of Elisha, in whose presence he receives the appeal. Either way, the king acts to *restore* what is rightly hers. The narrative attests that what the powerful are capable of taking is not in any case legitimate. This odd narrative attests that under the pressure of prophetic tradition, the ruling class can on occasion curb and redress confiscation, and so return land management to its proper shape.

3. *Usurpation.* The prophetic oracle of Mic 2:1–5 is an important marker in Old Testament teaching about the land that belongs to Yahweh. The oracle begins with "woe" (NRSV "alas"), which means "big trouble coming," big trouble coming in the normal workings of the order of creation. The indictment voiced by the prophet concerns sharp land dealings whereby the strong usurp the property of the weak. Micah, an agrarian protestor, has great suspicion about big-time urban operators who connive "at night" on their beds, phone their brokers at daybreak, and by noon have seized property. This action is apparently fully legal, but it violates the neighborhood and upsets the ordering of the land economy.[9]

The operational word in the prophetic oracle is "covet," which here does not refer to petty envy but to policies and practices of economic acquisitiveness that are, in a commodity-driven society, uncurbed. The target of such acquisitiveness is "houses

9. Reference to this process is the center of the many writings of Wendell Berry, as for example, *The Gift of Good Land*. Berry's novel, *Jayber Crow: A Novel*, is an account of the loss of ancestral land in the face of aggressive acquisitiveness.

and fields," the same word pair used to describe the loss of the woman in 2 Kgs 8:3. Micah the poet, moreover, refers to "house and field" as "inheritance," the tribal domain that is inalienable, but now usurped by acquisitive policy and practice that no longer honor old neighborly notions of the land. It is no wonder that the oracle of Micah continues with a harsh "therefore" of judgment in 2:3, anticipating a time to come when those who rapaciously seize the land of vulnerable neighbors are themselves vexed when Yahweh "alters the inheritance of my people" (2:4). Now the shift in "inheritance" concerns not just a few rural neighbors, but the whole of the land economy by foreign intervention. The oracle concludes in v. 5 with anticipation of a new "casting of lines" for land distribution, an assembly at the courthouse in which the "coveters" will not be permitted to participate. They will be excluded from the new land management!

4. *Arrogant Autonomy.* The three cases I have cited all refer to small local transactions wherein the urban commodity economy displaces the old tribal economy of inheritance, a displacement that characteristically goes under the rubric of "development." In citing Ezek 29:3-7, I move from conventional tribal conflict to the heady world of uncurbed superpowers. In the Old Testament, "Egypt" (along with Babylon) is a cipher for superpower pretension and posturing that assumes no theocentric limit to power. The upshot of the oracle of Ezekiel is that when Judah turns to Egypt for help against Babylon, Judah will find Egypt to be totally unreliable, a mere "staff of reed" with a broken body, i.e., strength that in fact is nothing more than unreliable weakness (vv. 6-7).

Our interest, however, is in the indictment of Egypt in v. 3 wherein the arrogant empire is condemned for saying, via its policies,

> My Nile is my own,
> I made it for myself.

Everyone knows that the Nile was there before Egypt, that the river is God's accomplishment, and that its reliability made Egyptian culture and power possible. But superpower arrogance has caused Pharaoh to misconstrue, and to invert the truth of creation. Rather than acknowledge that the Lord *made* the Nile that in turn *made* Egypt, Pharaoh can imagine he *made* the Nile. (The verb is a usual one for creation, *'asah*). Given that misconstrual, Egypt of course is not answerable to anyone, and so can use, abuse, exploit, distort, consume, and eventually destroy creation because the river is the crown's personal property.

But the indictment of the prophetic oracle that follows rejects the imperial claim of autonomy. Readers and preachers of this text amid U.S. superpower pretension will have little trouble transposing this oracle to "the last superpower" that imagines it can evoke "a new world order" to its own liking. Superpowers regularly refuse to learn about tenacious hold on the land that "colonies" continue to have, precisely because the land for them is never *possession* but always *inheritance*. It is for good reason that the prophets anticipate divine judgment on the superpower, a failed carcass to be fed to other creatures: "beasts of the land, birds of the air" (Ezek 29:5). In the end, Egypt will learn that "I am Yahweh," and that superpower status is fragile and penultimate (v. 6).

These conventional ways of acquisitiveness—eminent domain, confiscation, usurpation, and arrogant autonomy—violate the land that belongs to Yahweh and *not* to the king (1 Kings 21), *not* to the commodity traders (2 Kgs 8:1–6; Mic 2:1–5), and *not* to rapacious superpowers (Ezek 29:3).

To Control and to Possess?

Alongside these harsh denunciations of uncurbed acquisitiveness, I finish by citing three affirmations about the earth as guaranteed by the Creator:

1. "The meek shall inherit the earth." This familiar teaching in the Sermon on the Mount (Matt 5:5) is a quote from Ps 37:11, which is a sapiential meditation on the future of the land. Five times the psalm speaks of "inheriting the land," and alongside the "meek" in v. 11 refers to "those who wait for Yahweh" (v. 9), "the blessed by Yahweh" (v. 22), "the righteous" (v. 39), and those who "keep to his way" (v. 34) as the ones who will inherit the land. These various phrases all refer to Torah obedience, to those who conduct their life according to the well-being of the neighborhood as willed by the Creator who owns the land. The negative counterpoint is in each case "the wicked," those who advance themselves at the expense of the neighbor. This psalm, characteristic of wisdom teaching, attests that there are inviolate "givens" ordained in creation that cannot be safely transgressed. Among them is the maintenance of land through the practice of neighborliness.

2. The Decalogue, as is well known, concludes, "Thou shalt not covet" (Exod 20:17; Deut 5:21), a commandment that refers in these two verses to house, wife, field, or "anything that belongs to your neighbor." It cannot be unimportant that this command that curbs acquisitiveness concludes the Decalogue and stands in the position of final accent. The verb "covet" is the same one used in the indictment of Mic 2:2 (and rendered in Gen 3:6 as "desired"). The command and the prophetic indictment, as well as the creation narrative, understand that uncurbed desire will distort creation.[10] The commandment makes clear that, in the context of land management, all that is possible is not permissible.

3. In both Torah instruction and wisdom saying, the land inheritance of the vulnerable is inviolate:

---

10. Most remarkably, the catalogue of sins in Col 3:5 concludes "covetousness, which is idolatry." In this phrasing the writer gathers together the first commandment and the tenth, and indicates that it is in economic transactions that false gods are embraced and practiced.

> You must not move your neighbor's boundary marker,
> set up by former generations, on the property that will
> be allotted to you in the land that Yahweh your God is
> giving you to possess. (Deut 19:14)

> Do not remove an ancient landmark
>> or encroach on the fields of orphans,
> for their redeemer is strong;
>> he will plead their cause against you.
> (Prov 23:10–11; see 22:28)

The teachers in Israel can imagine that life is ordered by the Creator so that the strong and the weak may live together peaceably and justly. A violation of the entitlement of the vulnerable, by any violent practice, legal or military, violates creation and brings death.

Creation faith in the Old Testament links together the will of the awesome Creator and the well-being of the most vulnerable. Creation faith makes a claim that mocks our will to control and possess penultimate. That is, no doubt, why love of God the Creator regularly evolves into love of neighbor. Or, as the wisdom teacher has it,

> Those who mock the poor insult their Maker;
>> those who are glad at calamity will not go unpunished.
> (Prov 17:5)

Such a connection may give us pause as citizens of an aggressive superpower. Such connection makes honest preaching hazardous against the ideology of possessive autonomy, but for all that reason no less urgent. The question from Abner lingers: "To whom does the land belong?" Unlike Abner, we may entertain a reference point beyond the immediate conflict of "ours" and "theirs." Beyond any romanticism in Ps 24:1, there is a starchy insistence upon another landowner!

7

Remember, You are Dust

THE ASH WEDNESDAY GESTURE of ashes on one's forehead is
an odd act. On the one hand, it is so elemental and primitive, a
priestly act of rubbing charcoal on our faces.[1] On the other hand,
the act of ashes is indeed a freighted, sacramental gesture that
in one quick moment parades the whole of our life before our
eyes. There are no doubt good reasons (perhaps inchoate, but not
therefore less good) that the rite is steadily gaining credence in
"non-liturgical churches."

Dependent, Vulnerable, and Precarious

When the priest imposes ashes, the Bible is quoted: "Remember,
you are dust" (Gen 3:19). In quoting this passage, the church calls
to mind the entire narrative of the garden, and specifically, God's
decree concerning the serpent (Gen 3:14–15), the woman (v. 16),
and the man (vv. 17–19). Our verse is the culmination and climax

1. I will use the words "priestly, priest" rather than "ministerial, minister"
because I wish to underscore the sacramental character of the act of imposition
of ashes. In this act Reformed ministers are engaging in their proper priestly
act that mediates new life through the generative power of the liturgy.

of that awesome decree of judgment. Thus we begin our reflection with an *exegetical observation*.

Any text derived from Genesis 2–3 poses tricky interpretive questions, because the church's hearing of the text has been impaired by the overload of scholastic theology that is so present among us. Upon hearing such a text, our first instinct is to take the priestly formula as one more denunciation of sin, as though Ash Wednesday were a celebration of our sin and unworthiness. There are three reasons for hearing the formula as a statement of degradation.

First, the whole of Lent has been popularly defined as a season of guilt and penance, a period for confronting and acknowledging (and even wallowing in) our sinfulness. The sacramental history of the church (especially outside the Reformed tradition) has linked the journey of Jesus to the cross by stress on self-sacrifice, self-denial, self-abasement, and self-rejection. The "dust formula" easily serves such an agenda.

Second, the story of Genesis 2–3 is popularly and uncritically heard as an account of "original sin" and "The Fall." Classical theological exposition serves the propensity of popular piety just noted. In the face of such popular piety, it is exceedingly difficult to liberate the narrative of Genesis 2–3 from the imposed themes of "original sin" and "The Fall," even though few critical interpreters read the text in such a way.

Third, and more closely, our formula occurs at the end of God's speech of judgment (vv. 14–19) so that the text is heard as "remember, you are under curse."

Against the weight of popular piety informed by scholastic theology and uncritical sacramentalism, I shall argue that our "dust formula" is not a statement about curse, judgment, or indictment, so that the imposition of ashes is not related to guilt and sin. That is, the act of ashes is not primarily an act of penance.

It is plausible to suggest that our formula was an independent wisdom saying, a short, popular saying that urged reflection upon human mortality. When it is placed into this narrative, at the end of the decree of God, it forms a narrative *inclusio* with Gen 2:7, and no doubt refers back to that "formula of origin." Thus at the beginning (2:7) and at the end of this narrative (3:19), there are parallel, intentionally placed statements. The first narrates the way in which human persons have received life from the power of God:

> The Lord Yahweh forms (*ytsr*) the human person of the dust (*'apher*) of the ground and breathed into his nostrils the breath of life, and man became a living creature. (Gen 2:7)

This is a crucial and well-known text for understanding and articulating a biblical notion of human personhood. This formula affirms four matters: first, the human person is fundamentally and elementally material in origin and composition, genuinely an "earth-creature," subject to all the realities and limitations of materiality. Second, because the human person is an "earth-creature," it belongs with, to, and for the earth, and all other creatures share the same qualities of life. Third, this mass of earth ("dust") is no self-starter. In and of itself, it remains inanimate and lifeless. "Dust from the ground" by itself is no human person. Fourth, the vitality of the human person depends on God's gift of breath, which is freely and graciously given without cause, but which never becomes the property or possession of the human person.

Thus human persons are dependent, vulnerable, and precarious, relying in each moment on the gracious gift of breath that makes human life possible. Moreover, this precarious condition is definitional for human existence, marking the human person from the very first moment of existence. That is, human vulnerability is not late, not chosen, not punishment, not an aberration, not related to sin. It belongs to the healthy, original characterization of human personhood in relation to God. This is what it means to be human. This rather elemental and straightforward physiology marks the human person as a creature who lives by the daily, moment by moment generosity of God.

The narrative of Genesis 2–3 concerns the risk of trying to escape or transcend the modest status of creatureliness, the dangerous venture of "being like God" (3:4). When we arrive at the end of the narrative, it is as though the conclusion of 3:19 tersely footnotes 2:7, as though the narrative says: "See 2:7 above for a true characterization of human reality." Thus the movement of the human drama in this narrative is in three steps:

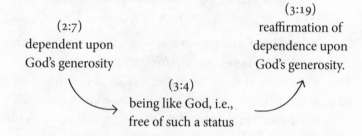

(2:7)
dependent upon
God's generosity

(3:19)
reaffirmation of
dependence upon
God's generosity.

(3:4)
being like God, i.e.,
free of such a status

Nothing about this precarious status is changed through the narrative. At the end of the narrative, the human person is as at the beginning. In the narrative, the human person seeks for and yearns for another status; at the end of the narrative, however, an alternative status is found to be impossible. The human person cannot escape the role of creatureliness given at the beginning of the narrative. Thus in the Ash Wednesday formula, the summons is not to acknowledge sin, guilt, and penance, but it is a call to *definitional creatureliness*, which in the middle of our life, as in the middle of the narrative, we tend to forget and seek to override.

Rethinking Our True Identity

The "dust formula" provides material for *fresh theological reflection*. The Ash Wednesday gesture is an invitation to rethink our true identity as a creature of God, kept alive by God's good gift of breath (cf. Ps 104:29–30). I suggest two theological facets to this narrative that are closely tied to each other.

First, the formula invites a theological reconsideration of human personhood (that is, theological anthropology). In our busy, anxious, and loud society, this reconsideration is a precious moment that needs to be guarded and nourished. We are invited by this formula to reaffirm our fundamental creatureliness, a creature of God wrought in and through God's fidelity. The Genesis story suggests that human creatureliness *vis-à-vis* God involves, (a) work to do *under a command:* Human creatureliness means to accept the work of caring for the garden, to till it and keep it. (b) *An uncompromising prohibition*, to refrain from the tree of good and evil, that is, to resist the kind of ambition that seeks to make us like God. Human creatureliness means to honor boundaries and limits that are not the limits of ignorance, but the limits of obedience and awe. (c) A *massive, genuine permit* to share the whole goodness of creation: "You may freely eat of every tree of the garden." True creatureliness means to be situated in the fabric of the life-support system of creation that makes our life not only possible, but good, whole, and abundant.

To recall our creatureliness is to affirm *the command* of responsibility, *the prohibition* at the boundaries, and the *permit* of generosity that envelops all of our life. All of this goes with being God's breathed on dust.

The second theme for our Lenten reflection is theology proper;[2] Ash Wednesday is a day for pondering God. Specifically, I suggest the theological text most closely linked to our "dust for-

2. The connection of the two themes, reconsideration of human personhood and pondering God, makes an argument arranged in the same way John Calvin begins his theological exposition: "Nearly all the wisdom we possess, that is to say, true and sound wisdom, consists in two parts: the knowledge of God and of ourselves. But, while joined by many bonds, which one precedes and brings forth the other is not easy to discern . . . Accordingly, the knowledge of ourselves not only arouses us to seek God, but also, as it were, leads us by the hand to find him" (book I, chapter 1). Calvin, *Institutes of the Christian Religion*, 35–37.

mula" is Psalm 103. We need to consider the whole psalm, but the connecting part is v. 14:

> God knows our frame,
> God remembers that we are dust.

The term for "dust" is the same as in Gen 2:7 and 3:19. More telling, the term we render "frame" is *yatsar*, our having been "formed." The noun is the same root as the verb "form" in Gen 2:7. Thus God remembers the way we have been formed in the beginning. Perhaps God, in this Psalm, remembers the narrative of Genesis 2–3, recalling the entire tale of our odd and awesome point of origin in the powerful generosity of God. Moreover, the verb "remember" is telling. A parallel to "remember" in Ps 103:14 is not found in the Genesis narrative, but in our Ash Wednesday formula. The word "remember" has introduced it into the liturgical formula derived from Gen 3:19, though the term is not in the text itself. We are invited in the gesture of ashes to remember. What we remember in Ash Wednesday is what God remembers in Psalm 103. We remember that we are dust, and God remembers that we are dust. In this Psalm, God recalls the narrative of origin, recalling how we were formed of dust, and now we are invited to recall this same narrative of origin.

This remembering on God's part evokes in God an act of gracious fidelity. The reality of our "dust" does not evoke in God rejection or judgment, but fidelity. In Ps 103:14 stands as a pivot point between two crucial affirmations about God. Just preceding this verse (vv. 11–13), human transgressions are noted by God and removed; they are made distant, removed as an immediate danger and threat. No big accent is placed on human sin. Human sin is acknowledged and then ignored. What counts is God's gracious act of removal. Concerning this removal, the poem utilizes two of the great words of the covenant tradition:

> So great is God's steadfast love (*chesed*) . . .

As a father pities (*racham*) children, so Yahweh pities (*racham*). When God remembers our dusty creatureliness, it evokes in God fidelity and compassion. God's loyal covenant love is the counterpoint to our dust.

Just following our pivotal v. 14, human finitude and mortality are recognized by God (vv. 15–18). God knows we are going to die, and this awareness evokes in God deep, caring concern:

> But the steadfast love (*chesed*) of Yahweh is from
>   everlasting to everlasting . . .
> and [Yahweh's] righteousness (*tsedeqah*) to children's children.

God's recognition of our transitorines evokes God's love and God's righteousness, God's resolve to right the world for us in ways that we cannot do for ourselves.

Thus Psalm 103 surrounds our "dust" with all of God's massive faithful power. The rhetorical map of our human dust is shaped in this way in this psalm:

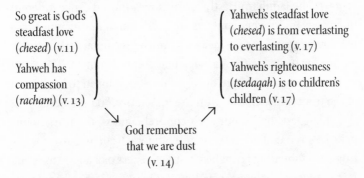

So great is God's
steadfast love
(*chesed*) (v.11)

Yahweh has
compassion
(*racham*) (v. 13)

Yahweh's steadfast love
(*chesed*) is from everlasting
to everlasting (v. 17)

Yahweh's righteousness
(*tsedaqah*) is to children's
children (v. 17)

God remembers
that we are dust
(v. 14)

It is as though God fully recognizes our needfulness and responds with the giving of God's own self in faithfulness, compassion, and righteousness. Indeed, what is detailed in the psalm is what God already has done in Gen 2:7, in the primal "forming," which makes new life possible from dust. The psalm asserts that God endlessly continues the same work, "from everlasting to everlasting," "to children's children" (v. 17).

Thus when we "remember that we are dust," we are made freshly aware that along with our remembering, God is remembering and regarding, for this is a God who "forgives, heals, redeems, crowns, satisfies, and vindicates" (vv. 3–6). The memory of dust then does not diminish and denigrate and humiliate, but is rather an evangelical affirmation that as we own our true self, we are invited to a trusting embrace of the faithfulness and power of God mobilized for our well-being. As we face our true selves, we discern our true place before the God of mercy and righteousness who continues to give life as God has given life in our narrative of origin. Our life in this moment of dust is rearticulated and redescribed in the truth of the gospel.

Counteracting Forgetfulness

These exegetical and theological observations take on poignancy when brought into contact with *our contemporary sociocultural context*. The familiar priestly formula may indeed evoke different intentions in different contexts, and the church in different times has found many varied meanings in the formula. But for now, we are concerned with our particular cultural context. The priest says, "Remember, you are dust." What does it mean to be greeted at the front of the church with the imperative, "remember!"?

I suggest that in our sociocultural context, the priestly imperative "remember" intends to counteract our massive forgetting. Our forgetting is not just inattentiveness or a failure to recall. It is not just a careless aberration. Rather it is a large, shared propensity to amnesia that besets us all and is the inevitable outcome of the dominant values of our culture. The amnesia that besets us commonly is sanctioned by our Enlightenment mentality, which on the one hand has scuttled tradition, and on the other hand, has reduced treasured memory to flat facticity. The sanctions of the Enlightenment have been reinforced by the seductions of consumerism that leave us so satiated (or lusting to be satiated) in the present tense, so preoccupied with present well-being, that our present intensities serve as a narcotic against a defining past or a summoning future. What is forgotten among us are the very categories of identity and perception whereby we receive a possible humanness.

So think of the procession coming to the front of the church. It is in large part a parade of the numbed who tend to forget what is crucial to our humanness. The act of ashes is a poignant gesture of reappropriating what we have lost, a jarring of the sanctions of our recent history and the seductions of our current economics. I suggest that we commonly struggle with two crucial forgettings, clearly related to each other.

On the one hand, we are to remember *our forgotten creatureliness.* (In this assertion, notice how far we are away from accent on sin, guilt, and repentance). We have forgotten our story of origin and our source of humanness. We have forgotten "our frame," our being formed. In the most drastic recognition, we have forgotten our morality, the reality that we are going to die soon; of course, our technological gains reinforce our avoidance of the topic and truth of our life. We imagine that if we are smart enough and quick enough and strong enough, we can fend off such a destiny by our self-securing.

The loss of our creatureliness causes us to imagine that we are more powerful and more capable than we finally are. It is this forgetting, I submit, that lies behind the greed, selfishness, anxiety, and brutality that drives our common life. We imagine that we are free to take whatever we want and can get. We imagine that we are required to take whatever we can get, because there is no one to give us what we need. We imagine that fending off death, which we can do for ourselves and which we must do for ourselves, gives us rights of usurpation and privileges of confiscation from our brothers and sisters and from the creation all around us. In our amnesia, the very threat of death that we think we have overcome in fact haunts us and drives us in debilitating ways. In what we take to be our massive and effective resistance to death, we in fact succumb. We become creatures in the grasp of the power of death. Because of our amnesia, however, we do not notice our succumbing. We imagine that we have won, and thereby we distort and completely misperceive our life.

In our forgetting, we neglect not only our God-given fragility. We also lose track of our vocation. We are, as breathed on dust, called into the service and company of another, called to do a work other than our own. This creature, formed of dust, is entrusted with the garden, with all the animals, and with all living things. Our creatureliness binds us to the role of steward, friend, and companion of all other creatures who share our fragility. We are to guard their well-being and dignity. Forgetting our creatureliness entails forgetting our true place and rightful role in the world. Instead of caring for and guarding, we assume license to use, exploit, and oppress. We forget what is important about us and our creatureliness.

On the other hand, we *also forget what God remembers.* We are invited to remember not only what we must remember, but to remember what God unfailingly remembers. We are authorized in recalling our creatureliness, that we are a daily creature of this creator who is endlessly forming and continually breathing on, naming and summoning, guarding and feeding. That is, we remember again that our life, like v. 14 in Psalm 103, is surrounded behind and before by the *chesed* of Yahweh who wills for us more good than we can will for ourselves. In this poignant gesture of remembering, we reaffirm:

> That I belong—body and soul, in life and in death—not to myself but to my faithful Savior, Jesus Christ . . . that he protects me so well that without the will of my Father in heaven not a hair can fall from my head; indeed, that everything must fit for his purpose for my salvation . . .[3]

3. *Heidelberg Catechism,* 9.

The ashes are not a sign of abasement or degradation. They are rather a sign; we are marked with an alternative identity, consisting in the asymmetrical affirmation of fragile creator and faithful creature. Those ashes of remembering are a mark of Cain (cf. Gen 4:15), kept safe in a hostile world, a mark written on our hand in affirming whose we are and who we are (cf. Isa 44:5).

When we go back to the pew after this freighted moment, we are transformed. We have broken free of the sanctions of the Enlightenment and the seductions of consumerism. The moment is rather like a homecoming, when we "come down where we ought to be." Our foundational homelessness is overcome.[4] We are welcomed home, no less fragile, but embracing our fragility that is now surrounded by a large, holy fidelity. In this moment of palpable creatureliness, fragility is not a warrant for greedy self-serving. It is rather an invitation to trust in the governor of the garden, who frees us for our work in being for our fellow creatures.

Relinquishment and Receptivity

Our exegetical, theological, and sociological criticism all come finally to this powerful *moment of liturgical confrontation*. In good liturgy, the inchoate force of the act is always more powerful than our capacity to explain what we say and do.[5] What makes a sacrament into sacrament is that the act is not subject to our rational explanation of what happens. The act is characteristically fraught with surplus. This act of ashes is just such an act overflowing with surplus.

4. On the theme of homelessness, see Berger et al., *Homeless Mind*; and also Lash, *Easter in Ordinary*, 216, 228, 268, who builds upon the primal work of Martin Buber. See also Elliott, *A Home for the Homeless*, on 1 Peter.

5. It is exceedingly difficult, in my judgment, for those of us in the Reformed Tradition, to permit and acknowledge the surplus power of symbolic action that runs beyond and outside the categories of our theological containment. Nonetheless, such inchoate force is operative in such moments of priestly activity.

It is a simple act. In its priestly character, it has an impersonal dimension. The priest does not hug us or call us by name, but speaks with distanced severity. The act is not designed to make us feel better, but it is an act of magisterial redefinition. In this moment the priest rises to solemn authority, the authority to recharacterize and redefine our life. We are in the presence of the congregation, and in this moment, we are along with the priest, expected to do our own remembering as we have done our own forgetting. We do not remember for anyone else, but for ourselves alone. The act is so simple and direct. I am addressed in an imperative, an imperative that is singular in its address and force. I am given a formula that is at least three thousand years old, but we keep reiterating that formula. I am touched by a hand, a brushed marking, a sign linking me to morality and obedience, marked in ashes, marked by what is left of our "earthly remains" when we will have been discarded.

All of these rather ordinary gestures, however, combine and conspire with a piercing force to make this moment laden and dangerous. It is a moment of confrontation, of combat and assault, in which a battle is waged for my identity. Liturgy is the proximate source of alternative existence, and this is an ordinary act that begins for me something new, namely a creatureliness that I have either neglected or resisted.

A world of memory meets the world of consumerism.

A world of creatureliness counters the world of autonomy.

A world of fidelity impinges upon the world of homelessness.

In this priestly formula, I am driven back to origins, to embrace large intentions for me that override my small self-presentation. I am situated for a stunning moment in the large panorama of creation. My name and my duty and my well-being are confirmed. I need not any longer practice my resigned amnesia, because I am grasped by an identity that has long been written in this narrative of forming.

Then I must leave the moment of sacrament and the service and the holy place—to return to the "real world." Except I discover that this is *the real world*, the moment of truth, my truth, God's truth spoken over me. And I begin to notice that my "un-dusted" experience has a phony ring to it.

What has happened is not simply a smudge on my forehead. It is rather an awesome, visible sigh of freedom and dignity, fragility and home. While it is there—and it lingers there a long time, because I continue to feel the priestly finger carving the gospel on my skin—while it is there, I have this sensation of freedom and energy and courage, strength in weakness, exaltation in lowliness. I am destined for a life other than my own, which in the end is my own true life. That may be what is meant in our formula about dying and being raised to new life (cf. Rom 6:1–11). These are the *ashes of relinquishment*, of dying whereby my whole false identity is released. These are, at the same time, the *ashes of receptivity*, flooded with new life given on Friday by the Friday one,

> who forgives all your iniquities,
>> who heals all your diseases,
> who redeems your life from the Pit,
>> who crowns you with steadfast love and mercy,
> who satisfies you with good as long as you live . . . (Ps 103:3–5a)

This new life is now surrounded in and saturated by blessing, a life now capable of hosting a blessing and being a blessing.[6]

---

6. I am grateful to my colleague, A. Hale Schroer, for supplying me the materials that stimulated my thinking on the theme of this essay.

Bibliography

Alves, Rubem A. *Tomorrow's Child: Imagination, Creativity, and the Rebirth of Culture*. New York: Harper & Row, 1972.

Anderson, A. A. *The Book of Psalms*. Vol. 2. 1972. Reprinted, New Century Bible Commentary. Grand Rapids: Eerdmans, 1981.

Barth, Karl. *Fides Quaerens Intellectum: Anselm's Proof of the Existence of God in the Context of His Theological Scheme*. 1960. Reprinted, Pittsburgh Theological Monograph Series 2. Pittsburgh: Pickwick, 1985.

Berger, Peter L., et al. *The Homeless Mind: Modernization and Consciousness*. New York: Vintage, 1974.

Berry, Wendell. *The Gift of Good Land: Further Essays Cultural and Agricultural*. San Francisco: North Point, 1981.

———. *Jayber Crow: A Novel*. Washington, DC: Counterpoint, 2000.

Brueggemann, Walter. "Disciplines of Readiness." *Occasional Paper No. 1*. Theology and Worship Unit, Presbyterian Church (U.S.A.). Louisville, 1989.

———. "II Kings 18–19: The Legitimacy of a Sectarian Hermeneutic." *Horizons in Biblical Theology* 71 (June 1985) 1–42.

———. "Praise and the Psalms: A Politics of Glad Abandonment [2 parts]." *The Hymn: A Journal of Congregational Song* 43 (July 1992) 14–19; 43 (October 1992) 14–18.

———. *Praying the Psalms: Engaging Scripture and the Life of the Spirit*. 2nd ed. Eugene, OR: Cascade Books, 2007.

———. "Preaching to Exiles." *Journal for Preachers* 16 (Pentecost 1993) 3–15. Reprinted in *The Word Militant: Preaching a Decentering Word*, 132–46. Minneapolis: Fortress, 2008.

———. "A Shattered Transcendence? Exile and Restoration." In *Biblical Theology: Problems and Prospects*, edited by Steven J. Kraftchick et. al., 169–82. Nashville: Abingdon, 1995.

————. *The Spirituality of the Psalms*. Facets. Minneapolis: Fortress, 2002.

Calvin, John. *Commentary on the Book of Psalms II*. Grand Rapids: Baker, 1979.

————. *Institutes of the Christian Religion*. Edited by John T. McNeill. Library of Christian Classics 20. Philadelphia: Westminster, 1960.

Conrad, Edgar W. *Fear Not Warrior: A Study of 'al tira' Pericopes in the Hebrew Scriptures*. Brown Judaic Studies 75. Chico, CA: Scholars, 1985.

Crenshaw, James L. *Old Testament Wisdom: An Introduction*. Atlanta: John Knox, 1981.

————, editor. *Studies in Ancient Israelite Wisdom*. New York: Ktav, 1976.

Cushman, Robert E. *Faith Seeking Understanding*. Durham: Duke University Press, 1981.

Elliott, John H. *A Home for the Homeless: 1 Peter in Social-scientific Perspective*. Reprint, Eugene, OR: Wipf & Stock, 2005.

Fackenheim, Emil. *God's Presence in History: Jewish Affirmations and Philosophical Reflections*. New York: Harper & Row, 1972.

Fisch, Harold. *Poetry with a Purpose: Biblical Poetics and Interpretation*. Studies in Biblical Literature. Indianapolis: Indiana University Press, 1988.

Fukuyama, Francis. *The End of History and the Last Man*. New York: Free Press, 1992,

Gerstenberger, Erhard S. "Jeremiah's Complaints: Observations on Jer. 15:10–21." *JBL* 82 (1963) 393–408.

————. *Wesen und Herkunft des apodiktischer Rechts*. WMANT 20. 1965. Reprinted, Eugene, OR: Wipf & Stock, 2010.

Hauerwas, Stanley. "Will the Real Sectarian Stand Up?" *Theology Today* 44 (1987) 87–94.

Hazard, Paul. *The European Mind: The Critical Years 1680–1715*. New York: Fordham University Press, 1990.

The Heidelberg Catechism. Philadelphia: United Church Press, 1962.

Hermann, Judith Lewis. *Tauma and Recovery: The Aftermath of Violence—From Domestic Abuse to Political Terror*. New York: Basic Books, 1992.

Hillers, Delbert R. *Lamentations*. Anchor Bible 7A. Garden City, NY: Doubleday, 1972.

Janzen, J. Gerald. "Metaphor and Reality in Hosea 11." In *Society of Biblical Literature Seminar Papers, 1976*, 413–45. Missoula, MT: Scholars, 1976.

Kaufman, Gordon. *The Theological Imagination*. Philadelphia: Westminster, 1981.

Koch, Klaus. "Is There a Doctrine of Retribution in the Old Testament?" In *Theodicy in the Old Testament*, edited by James L. Crenshaw, 57–87. IRT 4. Philadelphia: Fortress, 1983.

Kraus, Hans-Joachim. *Psalms 60–150.* Translated by Hilton C. Oswald. Continental Commentaries. Minneapolis: Augsburg, 1989.

Lasch, Christopher. *The Culture of Narcissism.* New York: Norton, 1979.

Lash, Nicholas. *Easter in Ordinary: Reflections on Human Experience and the Knowledge of God.* Charlottesville: University Press of Virginia, 1988.

Lifton, Robert J. *The Broken Connection: On Death and the Continuity of Life.* New York: Simon & Schuster, 1979.

Lohfink, Norbert. *The Covenant Never Revoked: Biblical Reflections on Christian-Jewish Dialogue.* Translated by John J. Scullion. New York: Paulist, 1991.

MacIntyre, Alasdair. *Whose Justice? Which Rationality?* Notre Dame University of Notre Dame Press, 1988.

MacPherson, Crawford B. *The Political Theory of Possessive Individualism: Hobbes to Locke.* New York: Oxford University Press, 1962.

Miller, Patrick D. Jr. "In Praise and Thanksgiving." *Theology Today* 45 (1988) 180–88.

Mintz, Alan. *Hurban: Responses to Catastrophe in Hebrew Literature.* New York: Columbia University Press, 1984.

Newbigin, Lesslie. *Foolishness to the Greeks: The Gospel and Western Culture.* WCC Mission Series 6. Grand Rapids Eerdmans, 1986.

O'Day, Gail R. "Toward a Biblical Theology of Preaching." In *Listening to the Word: Studies in Honor of Fred B. Craddock,* edited by Gail R. O'Day and Thomas G. Long, 17–32. Nashville: Abingdon, 1993.

Polanyi, Karl. *The Great Transformation.* 1944. Reprinted, Boston: Beacon, 1985.

Rad, Gerhard von. *Wisdom in Israel.* Translated by James D. Martin. Nashville: Abingdon, 1972.

Ricoeur, Paul. "Biblical Hermeneutics." *Semeia* 4 (1975) 107–45.

Scarry, Elaine. *The Body of Pain: The Making and Unmaking of the World.* New York: Oxford University Press, 1985.

Sittler, Joseph. *Grace and Gravity: Reflections and Provocations.* Minneapolis: Augsburg, 1986.

Soelle, Dorothee. *Suffering.* Translated by Everett R. Kalin. Philadelphia: Fortress, 1975.

Toulmin, Stephen. *Cosmopolis: The Hidden Agenda of Modernity.* New York: Free Press, 1990.

United Presbyterian Church. *Brief Statement of Faith.* 1984.

Westermann, Claus. *Praise and Lament in the Psalms.* Translated by Keith R. Crim and Richard N. Soulen. Atlanta: John Knox, 1981.

―――. "The Way of the Promise through the Old Testament." In *The Old Testament and Christian Faith: A Theological Discussion*, edited by Bernhard W. Anderson, 200–224. New York: Harper & Row, 1963.

―――. *What Does the Old Testament Say about God?* Translated by Friedemann W. Golka. Atlanta: John Knox, 1979.

White, Lynn, Jr. "The Historical Roots of Our Ecological Crisis." *Science* 155 (1967) 1203–7.

Wybrow, Cameron. *The Bible, Baconism, and Mastery over Nature: The Old Testament and Its Modern Misreading.* American University Studies Series 7/112. New York: Lang, 1991.

Zimmerli, Walther. "Concerning the Structure of Old Testament Wisdom." In *Studies in Ancient Israelite Wisdom*, edited by James L. Crenshaw, 175–99. New York: Ktav, 1976.

―――. "The Place and Limit of Wisdom in the Framework of the Old Testament Theology." In *Studies in Ancient Israelite Wisdom*, edited by James L. Crenshaw, 314–26. New York: Ktav, 1976.

Index of Scripture

ॐ

Index of Names